THE NEW

English

Springer Spaniel

by

CHARLES S. GOODALL

and

JULIA GASOW

Second Printing–1974

HOWELL BOOK HOUSE Inc.
730 Fifth Avenue
New York, N.Y. 10019

Contents

SECTION I

GUN and FIELD SPRINGERS
by Charles S. Goodall

SECTION II

SHOW and OBEDIENCE SPRINGERS
by Julia Gasow

SPRINGERS ON THE COVER:

Top: Ch. Salilyn's Aristocrat. *Photo by Tauskey*
Below: Solo Event, winner 1940 Open All Age Stake.
          Photo by Percy Jones

Reproduction after etching by Ben Marshall (1767–1835), a noted British artist. Spaniels such as these were the early ancestors of present-day Springers, and were known at the time as Norfolk Spaniels, Springing Spaniels, and by other names appropriate to the locality or use.

SECTION I

Gun and Field Springers

by

Charles S. Goodall

Charles S. Goodall

"Chuck" Goodall has handled Springers to more than 140 wins in the field, and has served as co-judge at five National Spaniel Trials, and at more than 100 licensed trials.

Preface

THE AUTHOR of the Gun Dog and Field section of *The New English Springer Spaniel* is pleased to be associated with coauthor, Mrs. Fred Gasow, who has very graciously accepted the publisher's request to write the Show and Obedience sections of this book. Her long time interest and personal experience in breeding and showing English Springer Spaniels on the bench more than qualifies her for the difficult task she has undertaken.

The revision and updating of the gun dog section was a most pleasant assignment, and the author is very grateful for the offers of help which came from all sections of the country. Regretfully, all the materials submitted could not be incorporated into the text or pictorial portions since it would require several volumes to accommodate them. However, materials which appeared to emphasize the highlights of history, field training, and the use of English Springer Spaniels as gun dogs for the shooting man and woman have been used if the pictures were technically suitable for reproduction.

In Chapter 1, a serious effort has been made to record the names of solid leaders whose contributions have been noteworthy and lasting. Special pains have been taken to emphasize the ever-increasing role that American sportswomen are playing in the gun dog and trial activities of the breed. It is gratifying, indeed, to see women shooting over Springers and competing at local and national levels with men. It provides strong evidence that modern day breeders have not neglected the all important characteristic of good temperament as they have increased the nose, drive, and speed of field type Springer Spaniels. And let there be no doubt that improvements in these areas have been substantial in even so short a period as the last 25 years.

The field-bred English Springer Spaniel is a magnificent gun dog and the leading contender for title of best all-around gun dog. This firm opinion is based on more than 40 years of gunning over and close association with good representatives of each of the several breeds of hunting dogs. We suggest that nothing can equal the ability of a trained, field-bred, experienced Springer Spaniel on a tough shoot adjacent to water in any terrain, climate, or cover.

It is physically impossible to acknowledge the pictures, ideas, and factual information contributed by scores of Springer fanciers from all sections of the country, but it would be manifestly unfair not to list the names of those who contributed so much of their time and effort to make this book possible. The author does gratefully acknowledge the contributions of the following fanciers:

Mrs. Evelyn Bui, editor of *The Springer Bark*
Mr. and Mrs. Joseph Crooks, dedicated Springer people
Keith Erlander, a successful Welsh professional trainer and breeder
Mr. and Mrs. Cecil Gipson, substantial breeder-fanciers
Julius Farkus, successful New York state professional trainer and breeder
Mr. and Mrs. William Lane, substantial Michigan devotees
Mr. and Mrs. Donald Maher, Illinois-California club leaders
Mr. and Mrs. Robert Setron, Western leaders and breed supporters
Paul McClure, top wing shot and club leader
John M. Olin, breeder, benefactor and outstanding conservationist
Talbot Radcliffe, leading British breeder and devotee of the breed
Mr. and Mrs. Ronald Weston-Webb, outstanding British sports people
Ernest W. Wunderlich, outstanding American amateur and wing shot
Mrs. Zelda M. Goodall, who spent many "lost" weekends typing manuscripts, proofreading, making editorial criticism, and doing research in Chicago and Los Angeles libraries.

—Charles S. Goodall

GLOSSARY OF SPRINGER
HUNTING AND FIELD TRIAL TERMS

Blink: An extremely serious fault whereby a dog deliberately avoids game, often due to too much pressure in training.

Bolter: A Spaniel that departs from his handler and goes self-hunting (hunts for himself and not for, or with, his handler).

Cast: Has several meanings, but usually means the distance or depth which a hunting Spaniel penetrates the cover when quartering.

Cover: Vegetation in the area where one is hunting or working his dog.

Hard Mouth: A fault by a dog which injures game while in the act of retrieving.

Heel: The traditional command ordering a Spaniel to walk at handler's left heel if handler is a right-handed gunner.

Honor: Steadiness to both wing and shot of game flushed by brace mate in a trial or while hunting.

Hup: The traditional command ordering a Spaniel to sit.

Objectives: Clumps of brush or gamey looking cover which a good hunting Spaniel should investigate.

Pattern: The degree of perfection, or lack of same, which a Spaniel demonstrates while quartering.

Potter: Lingering or remaining too long on stale scent.

Punch Out: Action of a Spaniel with a poor hunting pattern which hunts straight out and away from his handler, instead of quartering.

Quartering: The desirable back-and-forth, windshield-wiper-like, design to both sides of his handler of the hunting Spaniel.

Runner: Game which chooses to run rather than flush. Often a cripple with broken wing.

Steady to Wing or to Flush: A Spaniel that stops instantly and remains motionless when it flushes game, or if a stray bird passes overhead.

Steady to Shot: The act whereby a Spaniel stops instantly (preferably sits) when gun is discharged.

Wild Flush: A bird that flushes or lifts some distance in front or to the side of a dog, usually out of gun range.

Work a Line, Trail Out, etc: Following the body or foot scent in cover or on ground to locate moving game.

Print from *The Gentleman's Recreation*, England, 1686.

1

Origin, History and Development of the English Springer Spaniel

THE ENGLISH SPRINGER SPANIEL, leading contender for the title of best all-around gun dog, is an ancient and respected breed whose ancestors can be traced back into the dim and distant reaches of time. Thus the sportsman who would be thoroughly equipped to train and use these fine dogs in the field should have basic knowledge of the breed's origin and early history as a means of attaining complete utilization of their many and great hunting talents.

There are several theories as to where the ancient parent stock of spaniel-type dogs originated. Some say they originated in Great Britain. The majority opinion, however, holds that they first came from Spain, as the breed name implies. This position is sustained by eminent authorities, the first of which was the French nobleman, Gaston de Foix (often called Gaston Phoebus). He wrote *Livre de Chasse* in 1387, most of which was reproduced in *The Master of Game,* written between the years 1406 and 1413 by Edward, second Duke of York, who wrote that spaniels were good hounds for the hawk and that even though they came from Spain, there were many in other countries. Further evidence of their distribution throughout Europe may be found in the statement of the late Freeman Lloyd, a 20th century sportsman-writer of note, who told the author (about 1934) that he had seen an Italian tapestry circa the 1st century A.D., which depicted a spaniel-type dog fawning at its master's feet.

Another noted authority who held with the Spanish origin theory was the excellent 16th century British scholar, Dr. John Caius, whose book *"Of Englishe Dogges",* a short treatise written in Latin and published in 1576, states: "Of gentile dogges serving the hauke, and first of the Spaniell called in Latine Hispaniolus, there be two sorts:

1. The first findeth game on the land.
2. The other findeth game on the water."

The good Doctor described the land spaniel as "one which spryngeth the birde and betrayth flight by pursuite." He elaborated further by adding, "the first kinde of such serve the Hauke, the second the net, or traine. The first kinde have no peculier names assigned unto them save onely that they be denominated after the byrde which by naturall appointment he is alloted to take, for the which consideration, some be called Dogges

1. For the Falcon
2. The Pheasant
3. The Partridge
4. And such like.

The common sort of people call them by one generall word, namely Spaniells, as though these kinde of Dogges came originally and first of all out of Spaine."

Dr. Caius then distinguished between the two kinds of land spaniels of that day, one of which flushed game and the other of which set or pointed its game. He described this type, which is generally considered to be the early ancestors of our present day Setters, by the Latin name of *"Index".* Dr. Caius' work was translated into English by Abraham Fleming at a later date.

Most of the reliable 20th century authorities on Spaniels attribute the origin of the breed to Spain. Such serious students of Spaniels as Maxwell Riddle, the late Henry Ferguson, Clarence Pfaffenberger, the late C. A. Phillips and R. Claude Cane hold with the Spanish origin theory. The late 19th century British writer, J. R. Walsh, who used the nom de plume "Stonehenge", wrote that he had no doubt that the sport of Hawking was known and practiced by the early Britons, but that the Roman invaders under Caesar in 55 B.C. were totally ignorant of the science. He stated further that the Romans, who began their occupation of the Isles in 43 A.D., learned the sport of Hawking from Britons and improved upon it by introducing the Land Spaniel, if not the Water Spaniel, too, to the country. Further evidence of the Spaniel's early residence in Britain is to be found in an ancient Welsh law of 300 A.D. and 942 A.D. which referred to them by breed name. Regardless of whether one accepts the Spanish origin theory, it's not too difficult to imagine the sports-minded rugged adventurers of Caesar's Roman legions "liberating" a few Spaniels in their conquest of Spain and taking them to Britain, even as soldiers in the great wars of the 20th century and earlier have done.

Numerous ancient authorities considered Spaniels as belonging to one of two distinct types. The larger group comprised the *Land Spaniels* (some flushed and some pointed their game). The flushers beat out, flushed and chased game for the Hawks or Hounds. If the mounted hunters were slow in arriving at the scene of the Hawks' kill, the Spaniels were known to attack and even eat the hawk and the kill. The setting types crouched to enable the hunter to cast or drop his net over the game, and occasionally the dog, too. The second type were the *Water Spaniels* which retrieved waterfowl and, sometimes, the arrow which missed its mark. These facts are well documented in early literature and art objects as the principal methods of hunting in the 14th, 15th, and 16th century.

This was all to change, however, with an invention of great significance in which the wheel lock firearm was replaced by the flintlock. This notable event occurred in France about 1630, and since it reduced the time lag between the trigger pull and the discharge of the projectiles from the muzzle, made it possible for sportsmen to engage in "flying shooting" (wing shooting). This piece was introduced into Britain in the late 17th century and without doubt was the beginning of the art of fine gun dog training. Trying to shoot over one or several couples of wild, uncontrolled Spaniels with any kind of gun would have been useless then as now. As a consequence Spaniels during the next 300 years were transformed from untrained, wild beaters, to smooth, polished gun dogs which must hunt within gun range and retrieve with a tender mouth in order to save the game for the table.

The Springer's evolution from a variety of local types, used exclusively to start game for the Hawk or Hound, to a gun dog which would accept training kindly, was an evolutionary one. Early type Spaniels were described by one 17th century writer as being of 13 different kinds. Those called Land Spaniels came in a variety of colors, sizes, and shapes, as we have seen in their manner of handling game. And it was not unusual to find two or even three types in the same litter. Small ones (under 25 pounds) came to be called *cocking spaniels,* while the larger ones were called *springing spaniels* or *setting spaniels.* The setting Spaniels undoubtedly were the ancestors of present day Setters.

Much was written about the middle age practice of crossing spaniel types with hounds, terriers, and even "mungrels". These early sportsmen were able, however, to maintain the basic hunting desire in their dogs. Markham, for instance, points it out in his *"Art of Fowling",* written in 1621. He says, " . . . it is the nature of every spaniell to hunt all manner of byrdes (though some with more earnestness and greediness) . . . and there then remaineth nothing but the accustoming the Dogge thereunto, and acquainting him with your minde and determination. . . ." Thomas Bewicke (1752–1828) confirmed Markham's opinion, and was, incidentally, the first writer to use the words Springer and Cocker in referring to specific type Spaniels. His beautiful woodcuts of the 25 different "breeds" of hunting dogs of his day illustrate Springers and Cockers in great detail.

The impact of the advent of the flintlock on Spaniels was tremendous; just as some hunted with more desire than others (Markham), some were more tractable and quickly learned to hunt to the gun and not for themselves. This is highly important and one reason why modern field strains outshine their bench-bred brothers. The hunting strains through the ages have been selected and bred not only for hunting desire, but also for their ability to accept training kindly.

The first real attempt to standardize the physical and mental characteristics of the Springer was made by the Boughey family, whose stud book dates back to 1812. Many present day Springers can be traced to Mop I, Mop II, and Frisk—early inmates of the Boughey's Aqualate Kennels in Shropshire.

Organized competitive sport for Spaniels began with the founding of "The Spaniel Club" in England in the late 19th century. They drew up standards for bench show (physical conformation) competition and shows were held. But as often happens where qualities other than working or functional abilities are the sole measure of perfection, much controversy arose because the show dogs could not face cover or hunt properly because of their short legs and long backs. As a consequence another club, The Sporting Spaniel Society, was organized to test Spaniels for their hunting ability. Soon both clubs were holding trials (the first one in January 1899). At the third or fourth event a Springer dog

Print from *The Gentleman's Recreation*, England, 1686.

named Tring beat a Clumber named Beechgrove Bee (after two previous losses to Bee) to become the first Springer trial winner.

In 1902, the English Kennel Club recognized the English Springer Spaniel officially as a breed. The first Springer field champion in the world was C. A. Phillips' Rivington Sam, whose blood still flows through the veins of many present day Springers. Sam was probably half Cocker.

The late, well informed U.S. sportsman, Edward D. Knight, sums up the early development of the breed as follows, "It can readily be seen that the fountainheads of Springerdom logically fall into four distinct classes:

1. Individuals of relatively pure ancestry whose pedigrees had been privately maintained for generations.
2. Similar individuals which came from strains which had been bred for years by private families concerning which no records had been maintained.
3. Individuals of unknown ancestry which had been picked up purely on the basis of type or performance.
4. Individuals resulting from planned matings where blood of other breeds was frankly infused for a definite purpose."

During the first quarter of the 20th century six great pivotal sources or fountainhead strains of Springer bloodlines were established in England, according to the late eminent Scotch authority, C. Mackay Sanderson. The patriarch to which each strain owes its origin is listed below. Most of the top field dogs in Britain and America today have one or more of these great stud dogs in their pedigree.

1. F. C. Velox Powder, whelped in 1903, by Randle ex Belle.
2. E. F. C. Rivington Sam, whelped in 1911, by Spot of Hagley ex Rivington Riband.
3. Denne Duke, whelped in 1908, by Bosh ex Daisy.
4. Dash of Hagley, whelped in 1905, by Dash ex Beulas.
5. Caistor Rex, whelped in 1908, by Bob ex Lively.
6. Cornwallis Cavalier, whelped in 1914, by Spot ex Beaney.

Sanderson reported to the author that in 1948 the line from Rivington Sam was the top line in Great Britain, in that half of the British Field Champions were direct descendants of Sam as well as a score of gun dogs. He considered the bloodlines of Dash of Hagley as runner-up to

Eng. FTC Rivington Sam, the first Springer Spaniel ever to become a field trial champion in any country. Many of the great field dogs are direct descendants of Sam, who was owned by C. A. Phillips and trained by James Thompson, both of Scotland.

Sam in the production of Field Champions and gun dogs, with Cornwallis Cavalier in number three position.

In the second quarter of the 20th Century dozens of names of British Springer owners, breeders, trainers, handlers and shooting people may be found in the gun dog literature of the day, some of whom were known to the author personally or by reputation. Some of these who contributed the most to the furtherance of the breed, either by perpetuating old or establishing new bloodlines, and by testing the quality of their breeding efforts through training Springers for the gun or the competitive sport of field trials, are most deserving of mention. They include: C. A. Phillips, James Colin, Ethel Thompson, William Humphrey, The Duke of Hamilton, Lorna Countess Howe, Selwyn Jones, Joe Greatorex, John Kent, John Forbes, Tom Laird, H. S. Lloyd, R. R. Kelland, Colonel F. H. B. Carrell, Captain Traherne, George Curle, Mason Prime, A. E. Curtis, George Clark, W. D. Edwards, Edgar Winter, L. D. Wigan, Miss D. Morland Hooper, and A. L. Trotter.

In the third quarter of the 20th century Britishers who contributed substantially to the continued development of the breed must include the names of Mr. and Mrs. R. B. Weston-Webb, who bred four Field Champions, plus a number of fine gun dogs. Both handle their own Springers for shooting and/or trials. Talbott Radcliffe, another prominent amateur handler and trainer, has bred four Field Champions as well as exporting a number of fine Springers to America to increase

England's outstanding Springer breeder, Talbot Radcliffe, who has exported a number of top Springers to the United States from his famous Saighton Kennels. Several of the Springers pictured here are now in this country.

The noted British amateurs, Mr. and Mrs. Ronald Weston-Webb, with English National Champion Meadowcourt Delea, Meadowcourt Judy and Meadowcourt Polly. Mrs. Weston-Webb trained and handled Polly to her field championship.

the number of Champions from his blood. Hal Jackson, R. N. Burton, and F. Thomas were other amateurs who made their mark during this period. F. George, Dr. Tom Davidson, and Major Peacock also attained prominence for their contribution to the sport and breed. The Messrs. E. and M. Ainsworth were the owners, and D. Munro the breeder, of the outstanding British stud dog of the period. Their great male Field Champion, Rivington Glensaugh Glean, sired eight or more in England plus several others which acquired the title in the U.S. The late W. G. Sheldon bred five Field Champions and was an earnest competitor in trials. Mrs. Margaret Pratt and Mrs. P. M. Badenach-Nicolson are distinguished members of the distaff in British Springer circles. Jack Davey bred and exported to America Wivenwood Willey, who won the U.S. National in 1966.

The encouragement given by British sportsmen to professional trainers accounts in part for the development of the Springer with great drive, speed and enthusiasm for hunting, with nose to match the speed

The famous British professional trainers, Keith and Jack Chudley, with four of their many trial winning Springers.

All breed gun dog professional trainer Peter Moxon ready to work two interested "students" in the rabbit pen. British trainers utilize domestic rabbits in steadying Springers to flush and shot.

and temperament to handle kindly. There have always been fine professionals in England and the present group continues this great tradition. Joe Greatorex probably heads the list during this period with almost 20 Field Champions—a half dozen National Champions and several Brace Championships to his credit. Andrew Wylie and his brother, J. S. Wylie, have produced a score of fine gun dogs and their share of Field Champions. The same applies to John MacQueen and his son, John, Jr., who are cousins of Larry MacQueen, a top U.S. professional. Jack and Keith Chudley, another team of brothers, have developed winning ways at their Harpersbrook Kennels and delight many owners with their smooth polished results. Way up in North Wales, Keath Erlandson has made a fine reputation in a dozen years. He handled five Springers to the field title and bred many good ones including a double U.S. National Field Champion and a double U.S. Amateur National Field Champion (Gwibernant Ganol and Gwibernant Gefni), both of whom are pictured elsewhere in this book. Another fine professional who loves Springers, but trains all breeds of gun dog, is also most handy with the pen. Peter Moxon writes a column on Springers and has produced a fine book on gun dog training.

Readers desiring information on Springer activity in other countries are referred to the well-written *The Popular Springer Spaniel* by Dorothy Morland Hooper, published by Popular Dogs Publishing Company, London.

British trainers have used rabbits to start their young Springers hunting and retrieving for at least 100 years. Several years ago the government instituted a program to eliminate rabbits because of the destruction to crops and agriculture inflicted by literally millions of rabbits. This was a serious obstacle which required indomitable British courage to overcome. They have successfully overcome this handicap, as one can see from the quality and quantity of Springers they export to the United States. The current scourge of hoof and mouth disease eliminated most of the trials in 1967, but this obstacle they will overcome, too.

The Springer in America

The Springer Spaniel arrived in America at an early date according to G. Mourt's *"Journal of the Beginning of the English Plantation at Plymouth,"* circa 1622. He said one of the Pilgrims had a "Spanell" which chased deer. *The Sportsman's Companion,* published in New York, circa 1780, describes several varieties as fine shooting dogs when carefully trained. In the last half of the 19th century the sporting litera-

William Humphrey with FTC Aughrim Flashing and Horsford Hale, who placed first and second in the first United States field trial for the breed. Flashing later became the first U.S. field trial champion.

Arthur P. Moecher, organizer of the first two Springer clubs in the Midwest. Moecher, pictured here with FTC Busy Bruning and winner Benno Bruning of Ashaba, organized the first group training class for Springer owners in the United States in 1932. —*Photo, Stabler.*

ture lists the names of more than fifty sportsmen who owned and used Spaniel gun dogs.

It was not, however, until 1910 that the first Springer was registered by the American Kennel Club—a bitch named Denne Lucy. In 1914, the Canadian Kennel Club registered a dog named Longbranch Teal. But the real popularity of the breed in the United States did not occur until Eudore Chevrier of Winnepeg shot over a fine Springer gun dog in 1920 named Longbranch Teal. Chevrier was so impressed with Teal's hunting ability that he began to import English-bred Springers in great quantity for resale to American sportsmen.

Chevrier, along with G. T. Wolfe, Hayes L. Lloyd, E. T. Marsh, W. H. Gardner, and other Canadians, founded the English Springer Spaniel Club of Canada in July, 1922, and the first American trial for the breed was held two months later near Winnepeg. One of the winners was Alderbury Drake, son of the great British field champion Dalshangan Dandy Boy (a grandson of the first British field champion, Rivington Sam). The author's experience in shooting over Alderbury Drake in the 1930s inspired his interest in Spaniels.

The first Springer club in the United States, the English Springer Spaniel Field Trial Association, was organized about 1922 by Samuel G. Allen, William Hutchenson, and the three illustrious Ferguson brothers, Walton, Jr., Henry, and Alfred of Fisher's Island, New York. These five sportsmen had on-the-ground-advice and counsel from William Humphries, owner of the famous Horsford Kennels in England. The first trial was held at Fisher's Island in October, 1924, and was won by Aughrim Flashing, owned by Humphries and later sold to Mrs. M. Walton Ferguson, Jr., to become the first United States Field Champion in 1929. In 1927, the American Kennel Club recognized this club as the "parent club" for the breed. Shortly thereafter "Standards and Regulations" for field trials and bench shows were established, modeled after their English counterpart.

The breed was advertised extensively in the 1930s and 1940s by such famous outdoor writers as Freeman Lloyd, Bob Becker, Will Judy, Maxwell Riddle, Gordon McQuary, and others. Their recognition of the breed's hunting talents did much to popularize it with United States hunters. Later on, such fine writers as William Brown, editor of *The American Field,* Henry Davis, Jack Baird, Joe Stetson, Mrs. Evelyn Monte, David Michael Duffy, and Arthur Swanson kept the sporting public well informed of the merits of the Springer, until his kind were found in American hunting fields and duck blinds by the thousands.

During the second quarter of the 20th century, the United States'

The Ferguson brothers organized the club that held the first U.S. field trial for Springers at Fishers Island, N.Y., in 1924. At left, Henry Ferguson with FTC Fleet of Falcon Hill. Below, Walton Ferguson, Jr. at left, with Dr. J. Wilson and Francis J. Squires, and the Springers, Dual Ch. Tedwyn's Trex (imp.) and Trex of Chancefield. Walton Ferguson became the president of Westminster Kennel Club in 1934.

pheasant population grew by leaps and bounds as a timely replacement of the ever-dwindling supply of native game birds. It was then that Springers found a real "home" on these shores. Some thirty field trial clubs were organized by upland game and waterfowl hunters and the breed was off and running. Stud Books maintained by the American Kennel Club and the American Field recorded the offspring of hundreds of top field dogs of imported and American-bred stock and these became readily available to hunters. Names of leading United States fanciers of field type Springers numbered in the hundreds, but it would be unfair not to particularly mention the names of those who contributed most substantially to the development of the breed in America.

In the East such early pioneers as the Fergusons, Dr. Sam Milbank, Harry I. Caesar, Buell Hollister, and Robert McLean were joined at a later date by such outstanding sportsmen as Dean Bedford, S. L. Hutcheson, A. M. Lewis, Richard Migel, Mrs. Evelyn Monte, Charles Greening, Joseph C. Quirk, Tom Gahagan, Edward Whitaker, Mrs. George Watson and daughters Betsy and Mrs. J. Kineon, B. B. Flick, R. L. Cook, George Brennan, Carl Shattuck, Dr. William Goodman, Bob Sommers, Hartwell Moore, Paul Thompson, Peter Garvan, Colonel Raymond Costabile, Harry Taylor, Joel Lovell, Mrs. Robert Shaw, and Albert Winslow. Men of the stature of Robert McLean and Sam Milbank merit especial recognition because of their leadership in the parent association and the National Clubs. Others, such as the Bedfords, the Watson sisters, the Hutchesons, and Joseph Quirk carried on extensive breeding programs with British and American stock.

The fine Eastern professionals of an early vintage include Will Sinclair, the Jr. and Sr. Jasper Briggs, Harry Cameron, William Witt, Alan Reid, and Adam Eccles. They were succeeded by the talented Larry and Stanley McQueen, Arthur Eakin, Luke Medlin, Julius Farkas, George Ladd, each of whom were experts at turning out smooth, polished field performers for the public. Lawrence McQueen has handled three Springers to their National Championship.

Middle Western sportsmen actively engaged in shooting over, breeding and competing in the trials include the pioneers, Arthur Moecher, who instituted the first training class for gun dog owners in America in 1932, B. F. Genty, John Harding, E. W. Wunderlich, Dr. Stuart Sowle, David Silberman, James Simpson, Jr., Ray Minette, George Sokup, Hugh Herdman, Fred Sehnert, Ted Mertes, Tom Vail, C. K. Hunter, E. J. Elting, Howard Messnard, Tom Stabbler, William Paschael, Julian Collins, and Lawrence Gillingham.

The noted professional trainer, David Lorenz, with double National Champion Gwibernant Ganol, owned by John T. Pirie. Lorenz handled Springers to three National Open Championships in 1964, '65 and '67.

Chicagoland professional Elmer Chick, who handled Springers to three successive National Championships. The five Springers pictured are all Field Champions. L. to r. they are: Saighton's Shah, Tillian Ticket, Redland Marked Well, Sulphur Creek Dotty and Carswell Bedelia.

Those actively engaged with the promotion and use of Springers of a more recent vintage include Edward Porges, James Dodson, John Buoy, Mr. and Mrs. P. D. Armour Jr., William Lane, Dan Langhans, Gordon Madsen, Donald and Betty Maher, Charles Mee, Dr. John Ripenhoff, Jim Ritchie, Keith Van Dusen, Mike Paracsi, Frank Zohrer, Steve Sebestyen, Roy French, John Olin, Joe Zbylski, Mrs. Barry Phelps, Leonard Aldrich, Wallace Crawford, John Braham, John Blanock, Ed. Abraham, Burton Bratburg, Mike Niklaus, Edward Luthman, Jack Redeman, Al Hric, Curtis Killaine, Tom Fuessel, Arthur Mayer, John Pirie, and Jerry Baker.

One of the reasons for the great popularity and growth of Spaniels in the Midwest has undoubtedly been the outstanding professional trainers who have always been available to serve the public. The venerable Martin Hogan, his two sons Frank and Jim, and his son-in-law David Lorenz and David Jr., represent a total of more than 200 years in the field. Others such as O. H. Kale, Clifford Wallace, Howard Messnar, Eugene Whelan had scores of winners, Wallace having won Nationals with both Springers and Retrievers. Post World War II men include Steve Studnicki with four National Champions, Elmore Chick, and David Lorenz with three each. Lem Scales and Clarence Wingate have won and placed in several National Opens. Other good professionals include Donald Brunn, Roland Madecky, and Lewis Craig.

Canadian amateurs of considerable note are Ted Haggis and George Webster, the latter having handled the first two National Amateur Champions. Leslie Bunker has also had considerable success with his Springers.

Far Western pioneer sportsmen who have been a constructive force in introducing Springers to the public include the names of Dr. Charles Sabin, Robert and Charles Bishop, Dr. Harry Shoot, Harry Leeding, Donald Speer, George Higgs, Donald Montgomery, George Elliott, Dr. Jack Dodson, R. O. Bequette, Otto Lion, R. E. Allen, Clarence Pfaffenberger, Edward Roller, Lee Caya, Val Dervin, Dr. Rex Baldwin, Brian Ingoldsby, Sam Inkley, Glen Shay, and Ed Wright.

Westerners of more recent times include such fine sportsmen as W. T. Gibson, Bob Setron, Cecil Gipson, Albert Klein, Louis Sterling, Donald Shooter, M. A. Featherstone, Edward Cole, Edward Hanks, Joseph Crooks, James Driskell, Paul McClure, Kenny Williams, David Scott, Louis and Evelyn Bui (she does a tremendous job publishing *The Springer Bark*), Dr. Marlowe Dittebrandt, Harold Jones, Leroy John-

The outstanding Illinois sportsman, John M. Olin, and one of his Retriever champions. Mr. Olin, known internationally for research and practical contribution to all facets of conservation at Nilo Farms, has produced and competed many fine Springers and Retrievers in local and national competition. He is owner of Saighton's Sizzler, winner of the 1971 and 1972 National Open Trials.

son, Jack Redman, Ralph Newton, Joe Larrieu, J. H. Boyle, Art Perle, Dr. and Mrs. C. A. Christensen, Charles Johnson, Paul Diegel, R. S. Renick, Aidan Rourke, Dick Lane, Clark Hughes, Jack Feeney, J. P. Alvestad and Calvin James.

Recently Texas sportsmen who believe that the Springer can serve a useful purpose as a gun dog in that spacious state have organized a field club under the leadership of Carl Tate, Fred Pontello, Joe Reese, and Ed. Pomykal.

Western professional trainers who specialized on Springers were: Roy Gonia, Roy Wallace, O. H. Kale, Bob Sanchez, Bob Croft, Paul Ruddick, Dave Brown, Harry Mitchell. Brown, Croft, and Wallace are still actively turning out fine gun dogs.

Two events of the post World War II period greatly increased interest in Spanieling and also contributed a valuable by-product for the hunting man.

The first U.S. National Championship Field Trial was held in 1947 at the Crab Orchard Fish and Wild Life Federal Game Refuge at Carbondale-Marion, Illinois. Large entries in local trials resulted as sportsmen in 30 states attempted to qualify for "The National". Many fine dogs were imported as contestants and stud dogs as hundreds of sportsmen made their pitch to compete in this glamorous but highly practical event. This influx of new blood from England and Scotland created a reservoir of field dog Spaniels readily available for U.S. hunters. Sportsmen who joined the author in ten years of effort to secure approval for the first "National" were Bob Becker, Robert Bishop, William Kirkland, Dr. Charles Sabin, Conway Olmsted, James Simpson, Jr., and Harry Shoot. Factual proof of the field-bred Springer Spaniel's tractability and willingness to accept training kindly may be found in the fact that some 14 amateur handlers placed in the first 22 National Trials, with the 1960 event being won by a lady handler, Mrs. Julia Armour of Chicago. We doubt that any other breed has had so many successful amateurs appear in the winning circle in National field competition.

The Springers that have won the National Open Trials, together with names of their owners and handlers, are listed on the following page for the edification of breeders desiring to trace bloodlines:

WINNERS OF THE NATIONAL OPEN

Year:	The Springer:	The Handler:	The Owner:
1947	Russet of Middle Field	Roy Gonia, Wash.	Dr. Chas. Sabin
1948	Stoneybroke Sheer Bliss	Clifford H. Wallace, Ill.	Mr. & Mrs. P. D. Armour
1949	Davellis Wager	Martin J. Hogan, Ill.	David B. Silberman
1950	Whittlemoor George (Imported)	Steve Studnicki, Ill.	Mr. & Mrs. P. D. Armour
1951	Flier's Ginger of Shady Glen	Arthur Eakin, Pa.	C. M. Kline
1952	Stubbliefield Ace High	Stanley Head, Calif.	W. R. Gibson
1953	Micklewood Scud (Imported)	Steve Studnicki, Ill.	Mr. & Mrs. P. D. Armour
1954	Ludlovian Bruce of Greenfair (Imported)	Larry McQueen, N.J.	Joseph C. Quirk
1955	Ludlovian Bruce of Greenfair (Imported)	Larry McQueen, N.J.	Joseph C. Quirk
1956	Micklewood Scud (Imported)	Steve Studnicki, Ill.	Mr. & Mrs. P. D. Armour
1957	Staindrop Breckonhill Chip	Elmer Chick, Ill.	Rux-Roy Kennels
1958	Staindrop Breckonhill Chip	Elmer Chick, Ill.	Rux-Roy Kennels
1959	Brackenbank Tangle (Imported)	Elmer Chick, Ill.	E. W. Wunderlich
1960	Carswell Contessa (Imported)	Mrs. Julia Armour, Ill.	Mr. & Mrs. P. D. Armour
1961	Armforth's Micklewood Dan	Steve Studnicki, Ill.	Mr. & Mrs. P. D. Armour
1962	Kansan	Lem Scales, Kansas	Roy E. French
1963	Waveway's Wilderness Maeve	Clarence Wingate, Mich.	Mrs. & Mrs. William Lane
1964	Gwibernaut Ganol (Imported)	David Lorenz, Ill.	John T. Pirie, Jr.
1965	Gwibernaut Ganol (Imported)	David Lorenz, Ill.	John T. Pirie, Jr.
1966	Wivenwood Willie (Imported)	Larry McQueen, N.J.	Dean Bedford
1967	Brackenbriar Snapshot	David Lorenz, Ill.	Brackenbriar Kennels
1968	Tillan Ticket	Elmer Chick, Ill.	Charles Mee
1969	Dansmirth's Gunshot	Daniel K. Langhans, Ill.	Daniel K. Langhans
1970	Saighton's Sizzler	Clifford H. Wallace, Ill.	John M. Olin
1971	Saighton's Sizzler	Clifford H. Wallace, Ill.	John M. Olin
1972	Dot of Charel	David Lorenz, Ill.	Charles T. Curdy
1973	Dewfield Brickclose Flint	Dr. C. A. Christensen, Ill.	Dr. C. A. Christensen

National Amateur Field Champion Sunray of Chrishall, winner of six consecutive first place awards including the National Amateur Championship in December 1973, with owner/handler Dr. Warren A. Wunderlich of Joliet, Illinois. Sunray is by the noted British Springer, Hales Smut, out of Layerbrook Dusty Susan.

Dr. C. A. Christensen of Portland, Oregon, with 1973 National Open Field Champion Dewfield Brickclose Flint. This British-bred Springer is a sensational performer, with a great temperament that manifests itself in a strong desire to please.

Winner of the first United States National Open championship in 1947 was Russet of Middle Field, owned by Dr. Charles Sabin, and handled by Roy Gonia.

Davellis Wager, winner of the 1949 National Open championship, owned by David B. Silberman and handled by Martin J. Hogan.

Mrs. P. D. Armour, Jr. prepares to accept delivery of pheasant from National Champion Carswell Contessa. Judge Robert McLean observes the action. Mrs. Armour is the only woman handler in history to win a Springer National in any country.—*Photo, Shafer.*

Lawrence MacQueen, a third generation professional trainer, with FTC Jonkit Joel. Two of MacQueen's cousins are professionals in England. All three have great talent as gun dog trainers.

U.S. National Field Champion Brackenbank Tangle demonstrates perfect carry of shot pheasant as he delivers to E. W. Wunderlich. Tangle's win record of 11 Opens and 16 additional Open Placements is a near record.—*Photo, Shafer.*

FTC Micklewood Scud, an English import, winner of the 1956 National Open. Owned by Mr. and Mrs. P. D. Armour, and handled by Steve Studnicki.—*Shafer*

The second event that was to have a stimulating effect on the breed and provide more and better shooting dogs for the hunting man was the National Amateur Shooting Dog Stake. The first event was held in 1954 due to the great effort of James R. Dodson. It was replaced after a few years by the National Amateur Championship, modeled along the same lines as the National Open Championship, when Dodson and other leaders recognized the superiority of this type of competitive test.

The first National Amateur trial was held in 1963 and was an immediate success, being well supported by amateurs from all sections of the United States. In 1967, Mrs. Janet Christensen of Portland, Oregon became the first handler to place in both the Open and Amateur Nationals in the same year. Dr. John Riepenhoff's back-to-back wins of the National Amateur in 1967 and 1968, and then Daniel K. Langhans' sensational winning of both the Open and the Amateur Nationals in 1969 established new records for these events.

Winning Springers, owners and judges at the 1966 National Amateur Championship. Front row, *l to r.*: Curtin Killiane with winner Juliet Eb-Gar, Dan Langhans with runner up Dansmirth's Cricket, Ray Minette with 3rd place Talladego Tody, and Keith Van Dusen with 4th place Breckonhill Borderrange Bounce. Back row, *l. to r.*: Judges Arthur Mayer of Ohio and Edward Whitaker of Pennsylvania.

Winners of the Amateur title in the first years have been:

The year:	*The Springer:*	*The Owner-Handler:*
1963	Pam's Aphrodite of Camden	George Webster, Ontario, Can.
1964	Denalisunflo Sam	George Webster, Ontario, Can.
1965	Saighton's Swank (imported)	Jack Redman, Mt. Gilead, Ohio
1966	Juliet Eb-Gar	Curtis Killiane, Clarkston, Mich.
1967	Gwibernant Gefni (imported)	Dr. John Riepenhoff, Columbus, Ohio
1968	Gwibernant Gefni (imported)	Dr. John Riepenhoff, Columbus, Ohio
1969	Dansmirth's Gunshot	Daniel K. Langhans, Morton Grove, Ill.
1970	Misty Muffet	Mrs. Janet Christensen, Portland, Ore.
1971	Saighton's Signal	Dr. C. S. Christensen, Portland, Ore.
1972	Burtree Maverick	John Buoy, LaGrange, Ill. 246-0860
1973	Sunray of Chrishell	Dr. Warren A. Wunderlich, Joliet, Ill.

815-729-2970

Jack Redeman, of Ohio, with National Amateur Champion Saightons Swank. Redeman is also a wing shot of note.

Mrs. Janet Christensen and Juliet Le Grande, who she handled to placements in National Open and National Amateur Trials in successive weeks. Dr. Christensen is also a top amateur trainer and handler, and is the owner-handler of the 1973 National Open winner, Dewfield Brickclose Flint.

Registration figures at The American Kennel Club and The American Field continue to indicate that the Springer is much at home in America and that his kind, while never afflicted with the curse of extreme popularity that has been so detrimental to some breeds, will go on and on pleasing the hearts of the United States gunning fraternity for infinite years to come.

Robert Setron swings on a California cock pheasant as FTC Breckonhill Chance drops to flush.

2

The English Springer
as a Gun Dog

ONE of the most exciting experiences for a sportsman anywhere is to see a fine gun dog of any breed, well trained, well conditioned and with experience in the field, performing the things that he is capable of doing well. It's great and most satisfying, but the question frequently arises as to how the several types of gun dogs are supposed to perform.

The two great United States organizations which classify purebred dogs, The American Field and The American Kennel Club, have divided all purebred dogs into six groups, which are:

1. Sporting Dogs No. I (Retrievers, Spaniels and Pointing Dogs)
2. Sporting Dogs No. II (Hounds)
3. Working Dogs (Shepherds, Boxers, Collies, etc.)
4. Terriers (Fox, Irish, Bull, Airedales, etc.)
5. Toys (Chihuahuas, Pugs, Pekingese, Pomeranians, etc.)
6. Non-Sporting Dogs (Poodles, Bulldogs, Dalmatians, etc.).

There are more than 100 different recognized breeds in the six groups, but the hunting dogs (of which there are more than 35 distinct breeds) all fall into Group I or II. These are classified under four distinct headings based on their manner of hunting and handling game—the Hounds, the Spaniels, the Pointing Breeds, and the Retrievers. Hounds are the oldest and fall into two types—those which hunt and seek game with their nose (trail hounds) and those which hunt with their eyes (coursing hounds). Trail hounds such as Foxhounds, Bloodhounds, Beagles, et al, put their nose to the ground and search out game strictly with their nose. The sight or coursing hounds such as Greyhounds, Salukis, or Whippets search principally with their eyes and bring the game to the bag by their great speed.

The Spaniels such as English Springers and Cockers, called land or flushing Spaniels, search for game with their nose and flush (make it run or fly) when they come up on it. They are probably the second oldest hunting-breed type.

The Pointing dogs are of two main types: the older and more popular, the Pointer and the English Setter, and the so-called continental breeds, which are comprised among others of the Brittany Spaniel, the German Shorthaired Pointer, and the Wiemaraner. These dogs seek game with their nose and indicate it by freezing or "pointing" it when in close proximity.

The most popular Retriever breeds are typified by the Labrador Retriever, the Golden Retriever, and the Chesapeake Bay Retriever. They usually walk at heel or sit in a blind instead of searching in front of the gun, as do the several types of hunting dogs, and retrieve anything that is grassed or downed by the hunter. Each breed is a specialist and many sportsmen keep one or more of each type in his kennel. However, it is generally conceded by such noted authorities as Henry Davis, David Michael Duffy, and others who have had a world of experience with all types of gun dogs, that the English Springer Spaniel is a leading contender for the title of all around gun dog for the one-dog-sportsman who wants to hunt upland game and waterfowl. Having owned and shot over each of the several breeds for many years, we can only agree with the authorities—Spaniels are simply great.

The properly bred, well-trained and experienced Springer Spaniel, which has a 15 pound weight and strength advantage over his smaller cousin—the Cocker, is a joy to gun over. He should walk obediently at heel without leash, and when ordered to hunt will fairly explode, and always in the direction in which he is sent (right or left of the gunner). When he has cast 30–40 yards to the side, he will reverse his direction and whip back some 10–15 yards in front of his gunner at top speed. When he reaches the desired distance to either side of the hunter, he will again reverse direction and speed back in front of the hunter with great dash and hunting desire (almost as mechanically as the windshield wiper on an automobile). The Spaniel is a beater who covers all his ground to either side and in front of the handler, never leaving any game but always in gun range. When he strikes game (foot scent)

John T. Pirie, Jr. with FTC Gwibernant Ganol who won back-to-back National Open Trials to become a double National Field Trial Champion. Pirie's conviction that Springers are top gun dogs came after much experience with Hounds and Pointing dogs.

Cliff Wallace, Illinois professional, with National Open winner FTC Saighton's Sizzler, FTC Meadowcort Della, FTC Denali Mike's Mark and National Amateur Champion Saighton's Swank. Wallace trained and handled National Champion Springers and Retrievers.—*Photo, Daley.*

Mr. and Mrs. Harold Jones with FTC Sir Cricket after completing a series at a National Trial under judge Jim Dodson, who looks on from the left rear.

Lewis R. Craig of Ohio, and Steve Studnicki of Illinois. Craig is an outstandingly successful trainer and competent writer. Studnicki handled four Springers to National Open Championship.

he will drop his head and put his nose to the ground like a hound. He will persistently puzzle out the line (foot scent), increasing his speed as he approaches the bird or rabbit with his tail beating furiously and his animation quite visible. When his nose tells him that game is close, he will raise his head, take the body scent and drive in with a great rush that is guaranteed to drive it out from its hiding place.

Occasionally a wise old Dakota or California cock pheasant will leg it down the field so fast that the Spaniel may get out of gun range in his eagerness to flush. The properly trained individual will then respond to his handler's voice or whistle command and stop instantly. His veteran hunter will then move up rapidly to his Spaniel and cast him off again. The Spaniel will pick up the line of scent and again move rapidly in the direction of the game. Sometimes it will be necessary to stop the dog several times before he is close enough to flush. When this happens, he will hup (sit down or stand) instantly at the point of flush, automatically or in response to a voice or whistle command, and await further orders. If the game is shot, the Spaniel will mark the fall and retrieve it on command; if it is missed, he will resume hunting on command. If the game was only crippled, he will put his nose to the ground at the fall and trail it out with eagerness and dispatch—10 yards, 50, or 200—sieze it in his mouth with a gentle grip and return it to his owner's hand. An experienced, trained, and suitably bred dog of this type will not only fill the game bag but will provide many thrills and excitement for the hunting party. A real sportsman who thinks the hunt is equally as important as the quantity of game brought home will never hunt without a trained gun dog. The Springer is the pheasant dog par excellence.

Spaniels, and we include them all, even though we suggest that the English Springer has an advantage over his several cousins, provide great recreation and pleasure for thousands of lucky owners in several areas of sporting activity. First and foremost, there is the combination house pet and hunting dog of which there are many thousands in America. He will play with the kids, hunt a few pheasant or waterfowl, sleep by the fire, and make "Mama" comfortable by barking at strange night noises. Then there are the bench show types which compete and are judged on physical conformation (see Section two). When they acquire some 15 points in open competition they are awarded the title of **Champion.** Next there are the Spaniels which are trained to compete in field trials (simulated hunting). When they win two All Age Open Stakes or two Amateur Open Stakes they acquire the title of **Field Champion** (or) **Amateur Field Champion.** Lastly there are the spaniels

Bob Croft, leading West Coast all-breed professional gun dog trainer, accepts a retrieve from FTC Denalisunflo Dilly at a Stockton, California trial as judge Jack Dodson observes the action.—*Photo, Pearce.*

which compete in Obedience Trials. When they have acquired the proper score in competition they are awarded titles in ascending order of **Companion Dog, Companion Dog Excellent,** or **Utility Dog.** Each of the six titles indicates a distinct level of perfection, but there is no relationship between them. The Field Champions win on their ability to perform in the hunting field, the Champions are evaluated on their physical beauty and showmanship, and the Obedience winners receive an award for their ability to perform prescribed tests upon signal or command. The buyer should be aware of this in his selection of a puppy for a specific purpose. The several titles are awarded for excellence in strictly unrelated fields.

FTC Elysian Eric and Dual Ch. King Lion, the first two field trial champions on the West Coast.

Springers have a strong instinct to retrieve. Here is seven weeks old Waiterock Try fetching a California quail for owner Juanita Waite Howard.

3
Selection of a Prospective Gun Dog Puppy

A SUBJECT worthy of the effort is the first requisite in training an English Springer Spaniel to work to the gun. This is a most difficult situation to control, because most people acquire their first dog for reasons based on sentiment rather than on cold, hard logic. The best advice that can be given to one interested in acquiring a high class prospective gun dog is to go to the nearest professional field trainer in the vicinity and ask for the names of individuals who breed field type Springer Spaniels.

If it is not feasible to follow this suggestion, one should spend a month or two talking with friends who hunt, and try to locate a breeder who specializes in hunting or field trial stock. Advice of this sort is much easier to give than to follow, because there are numerous titles and championship certificates that can be acquired by an English Springer Spaniel these days that have no bearing on its ability to find game and accept training of the type necessary to produce a good field dog.

At the risk of incurring the undying enmity of Springer breeders who specialize in producing show type dogs, the author in all sincerity is compelled to say that Springer dogs primarily of show bloodlines are usually poor risks if one wants to have a really high class gun dog. Also, the Obedience titles C.D. or C.D.X. or U.D. mean only that the dogs have been trained to perform certain routine acts such as walking at heel, remaining in one spot on command, or carrying a wooden dumb-bell in its mouth while jumping over a hurdle, etc. There is nothing wrong with Obedience trials where dogs are tested on their ability to perform the above acts, and are graded according to their ability to do so. But there is no guarantee, however, or even suggestion, that a dog with these abilities (or its offspring) can scent a bird ten yards away, or exhibit an eagerness to crash into a duck pond on a chilly November day to retrieve a fat mallard drake that has fallen to the gun. The same facts hold true for puppies whelped from a mating of one or more show champions or from a bloodline of show champions.

The title of champion means only that the dog has near perfect body conformation and that its legs are straight, its coat the proper color and quality, its body formed in the manner prescribed by the breed Standard, and its ears the proper length, etc. It is basic logic to assume that Springers or their offspring which have been selected for these characteristics alone (this is true of most show strains), are not as well fitted to exhibit an overwhelming desire to hunt on a bitter cold day, or with the sun beating down in ninety-degree temperatures as occasionally happens during the dove shooting season, the partridge season, or in a good duck marsh. And of equal importance is the fact that show strain bloodlines have not been selected for the ability to accept training and to respond kindly, as have the Springers which have descended from hunting strains that are pure and proven for many generations.

Again, it must be repeated and stressed that there is nothing wrong with the sport of showing dogs, or the dogs that are shown, or the people that show them on the bench or in Obedience trials. Both sports provide a valuable form of recreation which is greatly needed in our most complex and high pressure society. It is wrong, however, to expect the son or daughter of a show champion or Obedience winner to develop into a high class shooting dog—just as it is wrong to expect the offspring of the best field dogs to do well or win at bench shows. The two types are as far apart as if they were two different breeds. And the occasional bench-bred Springer that does well in the field is the exception which proves the rule.

It is true that practically any breed of dog (or even cat) will hunt. The same applies to almost any other carnivorous animal because they have descended from long-forgotten ancestors that had to hunt in order to live. There is an amusing and apparently authentic case of a hog that was taught to hunt and, according to the writer, to "point" birds. However, the manner of hunting and the animal's aptitude—both physical and mental—to perform the job are most important, too. If one desires to acquire a saddle horse, it would be most unlikely that the offspring of a Percheron draft horse would be acceptable as a pleasure horse.

The highly successful New York professional trainer and breeder, Julius Farkas, introducing a 14-week-old puppy to his first "feathers". Note puppy's great interest in retrieving.

An eminent German zoologist who kept a number of dogs and other pets and who gained world-wide recognition for his studies in animal behavior, felt most strongly on the subject. He said that breeding and using animals for work (hunting, herding, guarding, etc.) was the only way to maintain the good qualities necessary for the specific action required. He said further that when the whims of fashion were the principal factors in determining a dog's appearance, the fate of the breed was sealed. Although the Herr doctor was not referring to hunting dogs in particular, it would seem that the general principle he laid down, of breeding for use rather than for appearance, would certainly be a case in point for selecting a gun dog puppy from hunting stock (bred for use) rather than from show stock (bred for appearance).

Mr. P. R. A. Moxon, a well-known English professional trainer and writer on gun dogs, sums up the subject of selecting a proper gun dog puppy prospect. He says: "Over here (*England—but it is equally true in the U.S., as most if not all U.S. amateur and professional trainers will agree*) there are two distinct types of Springers, and it seems that never the twain shall meet. I like the light-boned, fast, stylish type and have no time for the carthorse which our show people seem to love so much. The latter are far too big to deal with the sort of cover that Springers have to work in, and they lack working instinct and trainability."

Mr. Moxon has trained hundreds of dogs to the gun and his opinions are based on actual experience in the field with many, many individuals of both types. In the United States, professional trainers of the stature of C. H. Wallace and Martin J. Hogan arrived at the same conclusions. Likewise, such U.S. breeders as the late Colonel Joseph C. Quirk, of Connecticut, and C. K. Hunter, of Illinois, who produced winners in both bench and field, found that it required two distinct types to compete in the two phases of competition.

The chapter on the early history of the breed emphasizes that Springers and their ancestors had been used as hunting dogs for many, many centuries; also, that by the process of intelligent selection of stock having the talent or natural aptitude for field work, certain strains have been developed which could produce dogs with *extra* talent and ability for hunting.

The puppy selected as a potential gun dog should be from hunting stock. He should be the offspring of parents who have been owned and hunted by a man who takes his hunting seriously—or better still, from parents which have done well in field trials. This can be determined in part by a study of the five generation pedigree which most breeders are able to supply. High class gun dogs do not always appear, even from the proper breeding, but the percentage of success in producing high class hunting dogs is a great deal higher from field trial or hunting bred stock than from show stock. Perhaps as much as 100 to 1.

One should never forget that the gift puppy from the accidental breeding of some neighbor's Springer bitch, or the pet shop bargain at $15. may be a most expensive addition to the household. It costs just as much to feed and care for a poor specimen as it does for a good one, and it may cost a great deal more to train a poor one because it has not inherited the desirable qualities in enough intensity to enable it to accept its training kindly or to find birds easily. Then, too, the results may not be commensurate with the time, effort, and patience expended.

Clifford Wallace, of Wadsworth, Illinois, one of the really great trainers of Spaniels, Retrievers, and pointing dogs, has stated on many occasions that it is cheaper and easier on the trainer's nervous system to dispose of a poor prospect at once if it is lacking in any of the important qualities of a gun dog than to try to overcome the shortcomings with extra training. Thus, if a puppy eight or ten months of age indicates little or no desire to hunt or to retrieve after being exposed repeatedly to the opportunity to do so, give him to a friend for a house pet and get another one that will hunt and/or retrieve.

When the new puppy is acquired, the eminent animal behaviorist, Dr. Michael Fox, suggests that he be moved to his new home at six weeks of age, or at nine weeks of age. Because eight-week-old puppies are at a critical stage of mental and physical development, even a short trip by automobile or plane might prove traumatic.

Once a new puppy is acquired, stop at a good veterinarian on the way home and have the puppy inoculated with such homologous serum as the veterinarian may recommend. Repeat this practice religiously every two weeks for as long as the veterinarian may suggest until the dog has received its permanent distemper shots. It is also good sense to have it inoculated for hepatitis. Both of these diseases are great scourges and have been responsible for the death of many, many thousands of dogs. The author can state frankly that before distemper vaccine came into common use, over fifty percent of his young dogs died before reaching eighteen months of age. Since the advent of vaccination for distemper, not a single dog has been lost from the disease.

The puppy, once it is home, should be established in the place previously prepared for its living quarters. An outside kennel, with concrete or hard surface runs, is, of course, ideal when it is equipped with a tight, draft-free dog house. It is well to remember that a puppy can stand cold weather and can stand a certain amount of wet weather. It cannot, however, withstand both cold and wet weather at the same time. As most puppies have not the sense of older dogs, they will frequently play in the rain until thoroughly wet and then spend the night sleeping wet. An almost sure result is mixed infection, which can lead to dire consequences if proper steps are not taken immediately.

If the puppy is to be a house dog, a bed in a draft-free and out of the way spot in the house should be provided in advance. Immediate steps should be taken to housebreak the puppy. And any small children in the household, as well as adults, should be indoctrinated with the knowledge that little puppies require much sleep to maintain good health and cannot be played with all the time.

Remlyn's Tangle about to deliver a shot pheasant to owner-handler Remi Larrieu in California rice stubble.—*Photo, Bui.*

4

Preliminary Training
of the
Springer Gun Dog

T HIS CHAPTER covers the early phases of preliminary training for the gun. These may be classified under the headings of:

1. Retrieving
2. Introduction To Game
3. Basic Yard Work

Before training is begun, it is essential that the puppy become well acquainted with the trainer and that there be a feeling of mutual respect, trust, and regard between the trainer and his prospective pupil. This may be brought about by the trainer's doing most, if not all, of the feeding and grooming, required in the everyday care of the dog. Further progress along these lines can be made by the trainer if he takes the dog for airings and short walks (around the block), and devotes a few minutes each day to playing and romping with the young hopeful until a thorough attachment for each other has been formed between man and dog. Ten days should suffice for this phase. If a mutual attachment for each other has not been formed by the end of this period, perhaps the trainer has the wrong dog or his "get-acquainted" methods are incorrect.

1. Retrieving

Even though a Springer has a natural desire to retrieve, it is well to fix the habit of retrieving firmly before the dog learns to hunt. Springer puppies enjoy hunting more than retrieving and, if their instinct to retrieve is not aroused at an early age, may become more interested in finding a second bird to flush and chase than in retrieving the first one.

The first lesson in retrieving may be started with a puppy as young as three months of age. It may be done as follows: A clothespin, or a handkerchief knotted three or four times, will serve as the object to be retrieved. The puppy should be taken to a sheltered spot in the kennel yard, the basement, or garage and allowed to sniff around until all the strange new scents have been investigated. He may then be called to heel and teased with the object until his interest is aroused thoroughly. While the puppy is still interested in the object, it should be held just out of reach and tossed slowly three or four feet away. Eight puppies out of ten (Springer puppies, that is) will run immediately to the object, seize it, and with a little coaxing return immediately to the trainer. The puppy should then be rewarded with plenty of petting and friendly words.

Be careful not to throw the object more than four or five feet and always with a slow motion, as very young puppies cannot see very well and quick motions may be just a blur to their eyes. Repeat this performance six or eight times and then stop while the dog is still enjoying the game. Always reward the puppy with petting each time he performs properly. Eight or ten throws each day for a week will work wonders.

After the first day or two, give the command "Fetch!" in a firm but subdued tone of voice each time the object is thrown. This will form an association in the dog's mind of the article to be retrieved with the command "Fetch!" Never fool the puppy by failing to throw the object, and never indulge in a tug of war to get the object from his mouth. If his grip on the object is too firm, which is most likely, a little gentle pressure exerted by squeezing the lower lip against the teeth (on the side of the jaw) will usually induce the dog to release his grip. The command "Give!" should be repeated as this is done, in order to teach the dog to release the object. Don't forget to make a fuss over the dog and pet him profusely.

After a week or so, the trainer should clap his hands together to produce a single sharp report each time the object is thrown. This is preparation for introduction to the gun and is most important. Within a few days, the puppy will come to expect the noise each time the object is thrown.

To test the progress, clap the hands together sharply without throwing the object. If the groundwork has been laid properly, the puppy will whirl immediately and look for something to retrieve when the sound is heard. Again, do not fool the young dog. Always be sure there is something to retrieve each time a throwing motion, or the noise of the hand clap, or the command "Fetch!" is given. A child's cap pistol should be substituted for the hand clap after a week or two, when in the trainer's opinion the young prospect will not be alarmed by the noise.

The little guy will probably retrieve beautifully for a few days or even a few weeks and then suddenly refuse to bring the object to hand. This is normal behavior and it is also normal when he attempts to bury the retrieving object in the ground or under some leaves in the hedge. Sometimes the trainer can nip this undesirable behavior in the bud by making an exaggerated show of appearing to run away from the puppy, and thus causing him to run after the trainer with the object still in his mouth. If this subterfuge does not produce the desired reaction, one may attach a ten foot fishing line to the puppy's collar and bring him gently to heel with very, very light pressure on the fishing line after he has picked up the retrieving object.

These lessons should be continued for several weeks until they have been well learned and have become a habit. Little else should be taught during this period, and if the dog is to be kept in the house, the retrieving should not be started until he is well housebroken.

Older dogs can be started on their retrieving in the same manner if desired, although the retrieving may prove a little more difficult. Teasing and coaxing and holding the object just out of the dog's reach may have to be repeated a number of times with a dog as old as one year in order to arouse his interest. His reactions will be similar to those of the puppy except that he will be less playful.

The trainer must always remember to show his pleasure when the dog performs properly. Petting and speaking kindly with a friendly attitude are highly recommended. A reward of food, or some tidbit is a poor practice for a field dog and belongs more in the realm of the theatre than the field. The trained seal performs because he will be fed. A good gun dog performs because he loves it and wants to work for his master.

When the dog has become well conditioned to retrieving, a suitable retrieving buck should be substituted for the handkerchief or glove. If the prospect is under four months of age, the new retrieving object

Springer puppies should be taught to retrieve at an early age. Here Donald Maher's Square Peg's Rebel is shown at ten weeks of age picking up a feathered buck.

should be a tightly rolled piece of burlap approximately eight inches long and about two or three inches in diameter. It may be rolled tightly and secured by thick rubber bands. This retrieving bundle can be used until the dog is five months old. At that time, a retrieving buck with feathers attached should be substituted for the rolled burlap.

The feathered buck is made by securing a 12 or 14-inch piece of 2×2, and rounding off the edges. It should then be taken to the local tinsmith, and a light metal sleeve attached which will entirely surround the wood. Eight or ten pigeon wings, or the wings of game, or even of domestic birds such as chickens, should then be attached by a number of strong, heavy rubber bands. The young dog is introduced to the feather buck as preparation for retrieving birds later on. Most puppies will take to the buck immediately, but if the dog displays any reluctance, his interest may be aroused by teasing him with the buck held just out of reach. This must be repeated until the dog's interest is aroused thoroughly.

Always remember to repeat the command "Fetch!" *every* time the buck is thrown and to fire the cap pistol at the same time.

If the prospect is at least six months old, it would be well to introduce him also to the hard canvas retrieving buck, which is a small boat

Square Peg's Rebel, now a finished retriever, is shown delivering a shot pigeon to amateur trainer Donald J. Maher. Note the extreme caution Maher uses in handling the gun. It is "broken" and pointed away from the dog and his own body.

John Buoy of Chicago with five good Springer gun dogs at heel. Buoy divides his time successfully between piloting United Airline jets, training Springers, and shooting over them in trials and in the field.

Veteran Western sportsman, Don Shooter, with FTC Shooters Expiditus, one of the all-time West Coast trial winners.

bumper or fender stuffed with cork or kapok. It is well to get the dog acquainted with the new object, as it will be used in the water later. So the daily retrieving lessons should include the throwing of both feathered buck and the canvas buck.

One of the prime prerequisites of a good gun dog is that it retrieve with a soft and tender mouth. Starting young puppies to retrieve on a dead or shackled bird may sometimes result in the condition known as "hard mouth". This is a serious and objectionable fault and case-hardened offenders may ruin much of the game they retrieve by rendering it inedible. The method of teaching retrieving outlined above was first used in 1934 by A. P. Moecher. Using this method, a number of people have trained many, many dogs with good results.

After the dog has become well acclimated to the sound of the cap pistol, and has associated the sound with the act of retrieving, it is time to substitute a .22 caliber pistol for the cap gun. Blank cartridges should be used. It is most important to use the blank pistol with the act of retrieving. If the cap pistol has been used religiously, there will be no adverse reaction on the part of the dog the first time the .22 is substituted.

Take the dog to the training area in the field and work him on the feathered buck. Fire the .22 pistol the first time when the dog is some distance away on his journey to pick up the buck. If the noise appears to startle the dog, throw the buck even farther the next time, and be sure that the dog is 15 yards away before the pistol is fired. Two or three shots are enough the first time the transition is made from the cap gun to the .22 blank. If the dog appears to fear the noise, stop the shooting and go back to the cap gun for another week. The reason for this extreme caution will be explained in a later chapter.

If the noise appears not to bother the dog, the .22 may be used each time the dog retrieves until the sound has been heard at least 25 times. If no adverse reaction is observed, the trainer may gradually reduce the time interval between throwing the buck and firing the .22 until the shot is being fired while the dog is at heel. *Never* discharge the pistol over or in front of the dog. The gun should be held behind the trainer's back to eliminate muzzle blast in the dog's ears. Granted that a .22 does not make much noise, it is quite likely that no one has ever told the puppy this fact and his sensitive ears may find the sound objectionable if the piece is discharged in front of or directly over his head. This procedure is guaranteed to eliminate even the most remote chance of gun-shyness.

Considerable progress has now been made if the dog is responding properly to the various situations. If he is not responding, start all over with the early lessons and again follow the plan, step by step.

2. Introduction to Game

When the puppy has been retrieving to the sound of the .22 for at least two weeks, and is well adjusted to the noise, he should be taken to the field. One of the great advantages of owning a Springer is that he can be trained in a small area. The retrieving can be taught in a vacant lot and the dog's first introduction to game can be in a subdivision adjoining even our largest cities. Most areas of this sort in States where pheasants and rabbits are found will probably contain both varieties.

The puppy should be at least five or six months old when he makes his first trip afield. If he is much younger, he will have great difficulty negotiating the cover. The best time to work is early in the morning or twenty minutes before nightfall. Most species of game birds will be seeking the refuge of a weed patch in which to roost for the night and rabbits will just be starting to move about for their nightly forays in search of food and romance.

It is well to start the young dog out on rabbits because all dogs, regardless of breed, will invariably give chase to a fleeing rabbit, and Spaniels of all ages seem to have a particular fondness for them. The young hopeful who bumps into a rabbit or two and chases them by sight will no longer tag along at the trainer's heels but will be out in front hunting for more rabbits. When this time arrives, the young dog is making his first attempt to hunt.

Trips to the field should be scheduled as frequently as possible. If it is not possible to go daily, certainly Saturday and Sunday should be utilized fully. The early field sessions should not exceed 20 or 30 minutes time, but can be lengthened gradually as the dog's muscles develop and his wind and desire to run increase.

After he has chased a few rabbits, an effort should be made to bring the puppy into contact with pheasants or local game birds. Just before dark is an ideal time as the pheasants will sit tightly, and thus enable the dog to find and flush. If the first big cock that gets up startles him so that he does not chase, efforts should be made to encourage him to do so. The trainer should run after the bird for a few yards and exhibit great excitement. Most field-bred puppies will be off like a flash and chase the flying bird for at least a few yards—perhaps even as far as a few hundred yards. This experience on rabbits and pheasants or other game birds will speed up the puppy's hunting and increase his desire to find game.

It is more than likely that on future trips, the dog will dash away as soon as he is released at the edge of the cover and begin to use his nose as well as his eyes to find game. The position of the dog's head while hunting is a clue to the development of the hunting instinct. If his head is up and his neck is level with his body, the puppy is probably sight hunting. But if his head is down and his nose is to the ground, he is hunting by scent.

It should *always* be remembered, however, that the puppy must *always* be worked in the field with the wind blowing into the face of the trainer. There are two reasons for this:

1. It enables the puppy to scent game much better than when worked downwind (with the wind blowing on the back of the trainer's neck).
2. It will help, in most cases, to keep the puppy closer to the handler while he is working.

Once the puppy is hunting with enthusiasm and is beginning to appear bold and eager in the field, the early yard work can be commenced. It should be emphasized, however, that the retrieving lessons should be continued. Retrieving can be tried in the field but may result in the dog's ignoring the buck. Once the puppy learns to hunt, he may not be too interested in retrieving, except at home. This is normal and the retrieving should be given for five minutes at home before the trips afield.

If the trainer is unable to locate cover that contains rabbits and/or pheasants or other game birds, domestic pigeons will serve as a substitute. But better results will always be obtained by letting the young dog hunt wild game. Pigeons may be secured from farm boys or from the poultry market, and may be advertised occasionally in publications like the American Field. It is usually a good practice at first to place the pigeon (with flight feathers clipped) in cover and to let the young dog find it a few times. This will arouse the dog's interest and create much excitement on his part. He will catch the clipped-wing bird, and if the early retrieving work was done properly, will deliver it to hand. After two or three sessions with clipped-wing birds, the trainer can "plant" a few full-winged birds for the puppy to flush and chase.

Planting a pigeon is an easily learned skill. The method employed by many trainers is to grip the bird firmly over its wings with the right

PLANTING A PIGEON
The bird has been whirled and made dizzy. It is being planted in a nest made
by mashing down the cover.

An excellent close-up of Irving Puth "planting" a pheasant. Note the bird's
head tucked under its wing. When placed gently on the ground, the pheasant
will remain "asleep" for several seconds.

hand encircling the bird's body. Using lots of wrist action, the pigeon is then whirled rapidly for fifteen or twenty turns. The bird is then planted in the cover and will remain where it is placed. Best results are obtained by mashing down the cover into a nest approximately the size of the trainer's foot. This will permit the bird to flush without becoming entangled when the dog rushes in.

Some care must be taken in planting birds so the young dog will not learn to trail back to the bird by following the "bird planter's" footsteps. This may be prevented by walking in from the side of the area which the dog will work. One can also carry pigeons in the pocket of a game coat and "dizzy" them (as explained above) while the dog is hunting. The bird can then be thrown with considerable force into a spot of cover on the right while the dog is working to the left. Never let the dog see the bird planted. A little practice will develop considerable skill in planting by both methods and little or no difficulty should be experienced. Pigeons may also be planted by tucking their heads under one wing, then placing them gently in the grass. Pheasants should be planted in this manner. The dizzying method is usually better, however, for pigeons.

3. Basic Yard Work

The basic yard work consists of teaching the dog to **"hup"** (to sit), to **"stay"** (to remain sitting until ordered to move), and to **"come"** (to heel). The dog must respond to these three commands perfectly (both voice and whistle command) and continue these responses for the rest of his life. The importance of this early yard work, the ABC's of all types of training, cannot be overemphasized. The success of all future training hinges on the dog's learning to follow these basic commands. No hunting dog can be considered even second rate without this fundamental knowledge, and no gun dog can provide much pleasure, or function properly, until he has been so trained. These lessons must be learned well. They must be repeated at intervals during the lifetime of the dog and the better they are learned now, the fewer the problems that will arise in the future.

The old English trainers and some of the modern ones gave their gun dog puppies the early yard work before introducing them to game. Undoubtedly this sequence in the training procedure has great merit, especially in a country like England where there is greater concentration of game than in most sections of America. Teaching a young dog obedience usually curtails his enthusiasm to hunt, some more and some less. Because of the greater abundance of game, the English trainer can rekindle the enthusiasm to hunt after yard training much faster than most United States trainers. It is considered a better practice in America to have the young dog hunting and retrieving before he is given his early yard training. This is the reason for the sequence of training lessons suggested here.

Teaching a young dog to sit is an easy matter, but requires, on the part of the trainer, patience and a desire to succeed. In field work, it is customary for Spaniel owners now, as it was a hundred years ago, to use the command **"Hup!"** for the sitting act.

It is assumed that the young dog has acquired a good chain link "choke collar", and has made a good adjustment to wearing it. It is assumed, too, that the dog has learned from the early lessons to walk at heel on a loose leash, without tugging and pulling the trainer all over the countryside. If not, teach the dog to do so. Usually the dog will become accustomed to the collar if he spends a day in the house or kennel with the collar on his neck. A few strolls around the kennel yard or the block with a young dog held closely at heel on a short leash will teach him to walk quietly without pulling. The command **"Heel!"** should be repeated at regular intervals and be accompanied by a firm tug on the leash. If this mild restraint does not accomplish the desired results in five or six lessons, a small switch can be manipulated back and forth in front of the dog's nose on a line even with the trainer's leg in such a manner that the dog will receive a light tap on his nose if he attempts to forge ahead. This is a very easily learned lesson and one usually retained for life. In *all* his lessons it should be routine to reward the puppy by voice and by petting when he performs satisfactorily.

To teach the dog to sit, take him on a short leash to a quiet place in the garage or basement with no spectators or disturbing influences. Bring the dog to heel and give the command "Hup!" in a firm but quiet voice. At the same time, press down firmly but gently on the dog's rump, or hindquarters. Force him to sit, maintaining the pressure for five or six seconds. Then remove the pressure and at the command "Heel!," walk off a few steps with the dog still on the short leash. Then give the command "Hup!," stop, and press down on the dog's rump, again forcing him to assume the sitting position. Again maintain the pressure for five or six seconds, again repeat the command to "Heel!," and step off a few feet. Repeat this performance, but not more than ten or fifteen times at the first lesson. Gradually increase the length of time devoted

Mrs. Peter Garvin with her favorite gun dog, Denalisunflo Coffey, which she handles in trials and shoots over in the field. Both Mr. and Mrs. Garvin are ardent Springer fanciers.

at succeeding lessons until the dog is being worked for a period of ten or fifteen minutes daily. In a few days, the dog should begin to "hup", or sit, on command without the pressure of the trainer's hand. And within a week or ten days he should be letter perfect. The dog should be ordered to "hup!" every time he is fed, and should not be given the food until he responds. At other suitable occasions, the command should be given and the dog required to obey instantly. This command, followed by an immediate response by the dog, is extremely important. It should be learned well and obeyed without exception.

The next step in early yard work is to teach the dog to "stay". This is slightly more difficult and some young Springers do not learn it as fast as do others. It is relatively simple, however, if one is persistent and patient. The handler may start this training by taking the dog to a secluded training area in the yard or the basement and giving the command "Hup!." At the same time, the trainer should raise and extend the right arm upward with the palm outward and command in a stern voice "Stay . . . Stay . . . Stay", then take a step or two slowly backward while repeating the command. (In many cases, when he is commanded to "Hup" the dog will remain in position without being commanded to "Stay!". The trainer may then return to the dog while repeating the command "Stay!", and if the pupil has responded properly,

Western sportsman, R. S. Renick, with Cuttysark Fan Fan and FTC Cuttysark Trule Fair. Renick is a top amateur and sports leader.—*Photo, Dittebrandt.*

Edward Pomkal, Carl Tate and Fred Pontello, who have organized a Springer club in Texas in order to prove to fellow sportsmen that Springers are at home in any climate or type of cover.

he should be rewarded by petting and by voice. This procedure should be repeated ten or more times during the first lesson, with the trainer taking two or three slow steps backward from the dog.

In many cases, the puppy will learn what is required in a few lessons. He may not understand at first and if he attempts to follow the handler or move from the spot, the puppy should be picked up bodily and returned to the original spot where the command "Hup!" was given.

The distances may be lengthened gradually until the trainer can walk the length of the garage without having the puppy move. If it is deemed necessary, the learning process may be speeded up with a very mild form of punishment such as a chuck under the chin or a mild shake to indicate disapproval. One should never strike the dog, and by all means *never* lose his temper. Assume an attitude of patience, kindness, and firmness. If the trainer loses his temper or patience, the training session must cease at once and not be resumed for the rest of the day. A blow struck in anger may do irreparable damage to the young dog's spirit.

When the puppy is responding properly indoors, the lessons may be continued in the yard, and then in the field each time before the puppy is cast off to hunt. At the end of two weeks, enough progress should have been made to enable the trainer to "hup" the puppy, give the command "Stay!", and then walk in a complete circle around the puppy at a distance of fifteen yards or more. A puppy eight months old or more should demonstrate enough progress to make this possible with two weeks of training, provided the trainer has established a routine of working with him almost daily.

If the puppy does not appear able to grasp what is desired, another method may be employed in teaching the "stay". In this method a light sash cord or a length of nylon cord may be attached to the puppy's collar. The line should then be passed through a hook in the garage wall, around a tree in the yard, or around a stake in the ground. Upon giving the command "Hup!", the trainer can soon convince the dog that it is essential to remain in the sitting position. The choke collar will help with the learning process. Proper response to the command must be demanded. And following the foregoing procedure for ten or fifteen minutes a day for a week will get the idea over to the dog. He can then be worked with the line slack, although still attached to his collar. When the dog responds properly, reward him by petting and proceed with the lessons with the line attached, but lying on the floor. If the dog remains at the "stay" several times, remove the line and proceed with the lessons with the dog free of all restraint. Gradually lengthen the distance and, if the response is good, move outdoors first, then into the field, and repeat the lessons. Any slack in response is the cue to resume training the dog in the secluded area with, and then without, the line. To "stay" must become a firmly fixed habit in the dog's mind, so the lesson *must* be learned thoroughly. There can be no deviation from perfection in this lesson, regardless of the time required for training at this stage. Accomplishing the desired results will be well rewarded later.

The trainer should remember always to raise his right arm above the head with the palm outward every time the commands "Hup!" and "Stay!" are given. Within two or three weeks, it will be possible to make the dog "hup" and "stay" by merely raising the hand above the head. This is a most valuable hand signal which will prove useful in the field throughout the dog's life.

The third and final act of obedience the young dog should learn in early yard training is to come to the handler when commanded to do so, regardless of what he may be doing. This can be taught easily after the dog has learned to "sit" and "stay". It is done by again attacking the light cord to the collar and commanding the dog to "Hup!" and "Stay!". The handler can then walk away five or six yards and give the command "Come!" or "Heel!" in a firm voice. A gentle tug on the line will indicate to the puppy that he is to come to the trainer. When he does so, he should be rewarded with petting. This routine should be repeated over and over again for fifteen minutes each day until the dog has become thoroughly conditioned to respond properly. Usually the dog is so overjoyed at being permitted to come in for a pat or two that the "come" response is soon learned. As with the other two basic responses, it is most important to ingrain firmly the act of coming *each* and *every* time the command is given. No dog is a trained dog if he won't come each and every time he is called.

A word of caution must be given here to the over-conscientious trainer: Guard against overtraining the dog. Too frequent use of the commands may destroy the puppy's initiative and might cause him to stop hunting. It is necessary to mix a little common sense with the training routine and ease a bit if the young dog appears to be bored or intimidated. The wise trainer will observe the action of the dog's tail because much can be told by its action and position. If the puppy enjoys the work, and he certainly should, the tail will be up and in motion much of the time. If the tail is tucked between the legs and the puppy goes about his work with much casting of his eyes toward the trainer and without a considerable show of enthusiasm, the trainer is employing methods which are too severe. In such cases it is well to stop all training for a week or ten days and permit the prospect to regain his confidence by daily play periods. The training can then be resumed with the trainer using a more gentle voice and applying more petting and fussing over the dog when he has performed properly. Giving the commands too often in the field can result in a lack of enthusiasm for the entire business. Be sure that the dog *likes* the training, because serious problems can arise later if the prospect is cowed, or shows evidence of boredom or lack of confidence.

When there is evidence of considerable pleasure in performing all three actions, both in the yard and in the field, it is then the proper time to teach the dog to respond to all three acts at the command of a whistle.

One of the most suitable whistles, the Acme, is made of plastic and is available at most good sporting goods stores. It comes in three sizes but the smallest size is the most suitable. It is wise to purchase two or three whistles so that if one of them is lost, another will be available. A lanyard or whistle cord should be attached to each so they will be ready for instant use. The plastic whistle is preferable to the metal type as it won't stick to the tongue in cold weather or chip a tooth if the trainer should fall.

The whistle commands are readily learned and most dogs experience little or no trouble with the three basic commands. Most trainers use one sharp blast of the whistle to teach the dog to "hup", two sharp staccato-like blasts given close together to turn or change direction, and a series of short chirping notes to bring the dog in to heel.

To teach the dog to "hup" on the whistle, return to the secluded spot in the yard or garage and put him on the short leash again. Walk the dog at heel and follow the same procedure as was suggested previously when the dog was taught to "hup" on the voice command. A few minutes each day for a week is usually sufficient. After the dog is responding in the basement or garage, repeat the performance in the yard and then in the field before, after, and while the dog is working. Anything short of perfection here must not be tolerated, so, if necessary, return the dog to the yard several times to insure perfection.

In *extremely stubborn cases* where the dog refuses to respond, another method devised by Steve Studnicki, one of the top American trainers and handlers of fine Spaniel gun dogs, may be employed. This method requires the exercise of great judgment and *should be employed only as a last resort*. The trainer carries a small switch in his hand but keeps it well hidden from the dog by pressing it tightly against his leg on the opposite side from which the dog is heeled. The trainer then

Roy Minette with Amateur FTC Talledega Tody. Minette is a prominent Wisconsin sportsman who has been an officer in local and national Springer clubs many times.

Mr. and Mrs. William Lane with four of their field champions, and one near champion. Both of the Lanes have handled Springers to Amateur Champion titles, and their trainer, Clarence Wingate, handled one of their dogs to National Open Championship.

walks ten or fifteen paces and blows one sharp blast on the whistle. At the exact instant that the whistle is blown, the dog is tapped firmly on the rump by the trainer, who manipulates the switch behind his back. After the blow, the switch must be returned rapidly to the trainer's side in such a manner that the dog does not see it. The dog is then heeled and walked another few paces where the performance is repeated. It is essential that light taps be struck and the whistle be blown at the same instant. The purpose here is to condition the dog's reflexes with this bit of very mild force so that he comes to associate the whistle with mild punishment.

It should be understood thoroughly that there is no place in dog training for the application of excessive force, and the light taps described above should never cause pain. The purpose, more than anything else, is to startle the dog and to condition his reflexes so that he will "sit" quickly. Five lessons in which the tap is struck not more than five times, with two or three day intervals between lessons, is a desirable course. Even this mild application of force should not be used if it is possible to get the dog to respond without it. It should be used only in severe cases with overly bold puppies that will not respond to the more conservative methods.

The greatest fault displayed by most trainers is their effort to rush the training beyond the dog's capacity to absorb it. A puppy six months old has a very short span of attention. He may not remember things very long and cannot concentrate on any one thing for very long. He gets bored easily and cannot stand much nagging or hacking. So the lessons must be brief and to the point and must *always* be discontinued while the dog is still enthusiastic about the work. It is easy to break a puppy's spirit or to make him hate the training sessions. If the trainer is in doubt, the lesson should be stopped at once.

If the schedule of lessons recommended in this chapter has been followed, the trainer now has a puppy at least ten or twelve months of age that will "hup", "stay", and "come" on command. He will hunt and find game and can retrieve the bucks nicely in the yard or field. He will "hup" and come to heel on either voice or whistle command, and will also "hup" when he sees the handler give a hand sign by raising his arm over his head. The dog will walk on a loose leash without tugging and pulling, and by now even the trainer can see the results of his work. The young dog is now said to be yard trained and is ready for the more advanced work in the field and in the yard.

Bob Setron gives FTC Breckonhill Chance the hup whistle as Paul McClure, a top U.S. wing shot, prepares to swing on flushing pheasant. Chance almost caught the bird. Note tail feathers in his mouth.

5
Intermediate Field Work

THIS CHAPTER will be concerned with the intermediate field work, which, like the other phases of training, is of major importance. The main headings to be covered here will be:

1. Shooting Live Game
2. Quartering the Ground In the Proper Manner
3. Whistle Training
4. Steadiness To Shot and Wing

1. Shooting Live Game

Up to this point, little or nothing has been said about gun-shyness. There was a special reason for this, which can now be revealed. Many novice trainers do one of two things: (a) they either worry too much about introducing the young dog to the gun; or (b) they don't worry enough. It seems that there is no happy medium. It is the author's hope, therefore, that by avoiding the discussion of the problem prior to this point, his readers will consider the matter in its proper perspective.

Some of the early English books speak of gun-shyness, and certainly one who has had any association with dogs and hunting has seen many cases of this distressing reaction to gunshot. A pitiful sight indeed is the cringing, slinking, fear-ridden dog of any breed that has been *made* gun-shy by some unthinking or uninformed individual. The condition is produced entirely by man, for very few, if any, dogs are ever born gun-

Mrs. Betsy Watson and sister Mrs. J. Kineon, who breed and handle fine Springers in a kennel started by their parents 30 years ago. Both are excellent amateur handlers.—*Photo, Craig.*

Mrs. Evelyn Monte, prominent writer, amateur handler and judge of Springer and Pointing dogs, with George Webster, a successful Canadian Spaniel man.

shy. Usually, if one takes the trouble to investigate each case that comes to attention, some bit of man's stupidity or ignorance will be found to be responsible for the condition.

One of the worst cases ever observed was that of a nice Springer bitch who would practically go into convulsions, not only at the sound of a gun, but also at the sight of a broom or any other object which bore even a faint resemblance to a gun. Several of her littermates were good gun dogs and perhaps this bitch would have been, too, if she had not been taken to a gun club at the tender age of three months. When she first heard the sound of a 12 gauge gun, she cringed and exhibited some evidence of fear. After two hours of the same medicine, the dog was in a blue funk and a most pitiful sight. Her inexperienced owners erroneously attributed her condition to car sickness. A day or two later, when a .22 rifle was discharged at a starling in her owner's yard, the puppy learned, then and there, to associate the sound of the gun with its appearance and from then on would almost collapse from fright at either the sound or the sight of anything even faintly resembling a gun.

A second common cause of gun-shyness is the Fourth of July firecracker thrown at the puppy's feet by some thoughtless youngster. The burning fuse usually attracts the puppy's attention and if he attempts to seize the firecracker or to paw it, the results are sure and positive. The noise and the flash burn will condition the puppy adversely and gun-shyness is the result.

Young dogs may also become gun-shy by being shot over without the proper preparation.

Gun-shyness can be cured but it is a long, slow process. Months of re-education may be required to overcome the phobia. It is so easy to avoid this condition by proper early conditioning, that one is inclined to think that no space should be devoted to the cure. However, a procedure for overcoming this most serious fault will be suggested in the chapter on correcting faults in Springer gun dogs. No normal hunting dog can *ever* be made gun-shy by following the procedure outlined in this book unless the dog is subjected to other outside influences.

The thoughtful reader will recall the suggestion that a sharp hand clap be associated with the early retrieving lessons. It was also suggested that a cap pistol, and later a .22 blank pistol, be introduced gradually into the retrieving routine. It should come as no surprise, then, to learn that any dog that was conditioned by this method is safely past the gun and the introduction to the sound of shot. Therefore, taking him into the field and actually shooting several planted pigeons with a shotgun for the dog to retrieve is rather an anticlimax.

That, however, is the next step and is a procedure that should be repeated subsequently on five or six occasions. If the trainer is not an expert shot, a friend who is a good wing shot may be invited to do the actual shooting, for it is most important that the first few birds be downed for the dog to retrieve. It is preferable to use a light 20 gauge gun the first time or two, and, of course, the birds should be shot while the dog is giving chase.

Continue these lessons for several weeks until the dog is thoroughly habituated to the sound of the shotgun and exhibits enthusiasm every time he sees the gun. It is well to remember never to shoot at close range directly over the head of a dog or a human, as muzzle blast is rather severe and has been known to rupture the eardrum or induce temporary deafness.

2. Quartering the Ground

Not only must gun dogs of all breeds learn to hunt, but also they must learn to hunt in the places where game is most likely to be found. The big, wide-ranging, bird-wise Pointer or Setter will hunt the birdy places such as fence rows, where experience has taught that quail may be found. A Springer Spaniel will learn to work birdy places, too, but because he is a "flushing dog" and not a pointing dog, he must be trained to stay always within gun range. It is easy to see that the fast, keen, eager Springer will not stay within gun range unless taught to quarter back and forth in front of the handler. If the Springer is permitted to range out or punch out wide like a pointing dog, little or no game would be put up within gun range, because the Spaniel flushes birds instead of holding them by pointing. The trainer, then, must strive to make the young Spaniel quarter the ground in front of the gun in an almost mechanical manner. Later on, as the dog gains experience on game, he will break this rigid pattern occasionally, but he must be well grounded in the fundamentals of quartering first in order to produce the best results later.

An earlier chapter suggested that the young Springer always be worked into the wind. The reason for this procedure is to lay the groundwork for teaching the dog to quarter. In many young Springers of field breeding it appears to be an inherited characteristic to quarter almost automatically. When this is the case, the trainer's problem is relatively simple. All he need do is to widen the dog's hunting pattern some (encourage him to cast out as far as forty yards to either side of the trainer) and work the dog enough to make the quartering a habit.

If the dog has not started to quarter naturally, he may need some guidance in the matter. This can be accomplished by setting the puppy down at heel and by then sending him out to the right side with a wave of the hand and the command "Hi-on". If the wind is in the trainer's face, the young dog will usually not hunt straight ahead, anyway, and by giving him a wave to the right, he will most likely respond as required. If not, the trainer can repeat the signal and walk in that direction.

When the young dog has gone out 35 or 40 yards, the trainer can give *two* sharp toots of the whistle to attract his attention, and walk to the left. When the dog reaches the extreme limit of 40 yards on the cast to the left, the trainer can again give two sharp toots on the whistle and head in the opposite direction. Three or four lessons should get the idea over that he is to hunt out to either *side* of the trainer rather than straight out in front. It cannot be emphasized too much that the trainer must *always* walk into the wind in early field work. The wind alone is almost enough to cause the dog to hunt the pattern that all Spaniel trainers desire, but if it is not, the trainer must encourage the dog to quarter.

Although no previous reference was made to the procedure, the trainer should have devoted some time to hand signals in the early retrieving lessons. The purpose of hand signals is to direct the dog to a retrieve he has failed to mark and also to indicate where he is to hunt. When young puppies fail to mark the fall of the buck, the trainer should utilize these occasions to teach the dog to take hand signals by indicating the location of the buck with a wave of the hand. A few such experiences are usually enough to accustom the dog to the fact that if he hunts in the direction indicated by the trainer's hand signal, he will find the bird or buck promptly. Another most effective manner of teaching a dog to respond to hand signals is to plant a few birds to the extreme right or left of the imaginary line on which the trainer walks as he works the dog. If the trainer will have the dog into a half dozen or more live birds, it will speed up the learning process greatly.

3. Teaching the Dog to Turn on the Whistle

While the dog is learning to quarter his ground properly, the trainer should use the whistle as indicated previously. At first the dog will glance at the handler and probably follow directions as indicated by a wave of the hand. Eventually he will merely change his direction and when the two whistle toots are given, will hunt the other side of the handler, sometimes without looking for directions. If the dog is not responding to the whistle, the trainer can call out sternly, indicating that he means business. If this fails to produce the desired results, he should rush out rapidly and give the dog a brisk shake of the collar and sound two blasts of the whistle. A few such actions will make it clear that the dog must respond to the whistle signals. There are other methods, such as attaching a check cord to the dog's collar and forcing him to change directions when the whistle signal is given. Another method is to blow the "hup" whistle, which will cause the dog to stop (if the early training has been thorough), and, while the dog's attention is directed wholly to the trainer, then to indicate the direction in which the dog is to hunt. One, or a combination, of these techniques will produce the desired results.

It is the practice on the part of some trainers to use extreme force with stubborn cases, but such procedure is not recommended for the novice. Considerable judgment and skill are required if force is to be employed properly, and it is probable that more harm than good will result, even at the hands of an expert trainer. One can usually spot the force-trained dog, no matter whether he be retrieving, hunting, entering the water, etc. If, in learning to turn on the whistle, the dog does not respond to any of the foregoing methods, he can be stung by a marble discharged from a slingshot or by a pellet discharged from a BB gun in which the spring has been weakened. These methods are *not* recommended and are reported merely to indicate the steps that may be taken in extreme and severe cases. Years ago it was the custom of some trainers to fire a load of fine bird shot from a shotgun at a wilfully disobedient dog. Fortunately, this has been discontinued by the successful trainers.

Dogs that are *forced* to perform any of the acts required of good gun dogs never exhibit much spirit and animation, nor are they as dependable as those that are trained through constant repetition to perform the required acts. This statement is based on common sense, experience, and the findings of the animal behavior workers in the research departments of our leading universities. If by repetition a dog's reflexes become thoroughly conditioned to perform a certain act in a certain way, he often becomes a most dependable animal.

4. Steadying the Dog to Shot and Wing

One of the most important requirements of a good gun dog is that he be steady to shot and wing.

For those not familiar with the terminology, steadiness to shot and wing means that the dog will stop dead in his tracks and sit ("hup") at the instant that a bird is flushed or that a gun is discharged. The reasons for requiring a dog to react in this manner are both useful and practical. The following factual account of a South Dakota hunting trip illustrates the reason most vividly.

The hunting party in question was undertaken by three sportsmen who owned well-trained Spaniels and who were persuaded at the last minute to include the owner of an unsteady Spaniel in the party. When the group arrived in South Dakota and entered the first corn field, which was fairly alive with pheasants, the dogs were ordered to heel and the four hunters and their dogs proceeded down the corn rows about ten yards apart. About halfway through the field, one of the dogs dived through two rows of corn to flush a smart old cock that had squatted under some light cover, hoping that the hunters would pass him by. The bird flushed in front of the hunters and was dropped immediately by the center gun. The three steady dogs dropped to shot ("hupped") to await orders, while the unsteady Springer headed toward the "fall" to make the retrieve without command. He overran the "fall", proceeded down the field, and bumped into another pheasant which flushed immediately. He gave chase and within three minutes had flushed perhaps forty pheasants out of the corn, none of which came within gun range of the four hunters. No one had too much to say to the owner of the breaking dog, but a great deal of silent swearing took place.

Some of the birds that had been flushed were marked down in a slough about a half mile away. The four gunners headed in that direction with their dogs at heel. Upon entering the slough, which was a large one, all dogs were ordered to "Hi-on". As luck would have it, the unsteady dog flushed the first bird and took off on a wild chase. His actions again caused all the birds in the slough except one lone hen to flush out of gun range, and not one shot was fired, though a hundred or more birds had been in the vicinity of the hunters in the corn field and the slough.

A council of war was held immediately and, by vote of three to one, the unsteady dog was banished to the security of the automobile for the duration of the hunt. After this had transpired, the four hunters proceeded to work out some likely spots of cover and, with the help of three trained dogs, were able in a few hours to take their daily limit. The first hour of the hunt produced one bird for the bag, the next three hours produced twenty-seven which were flushed and retrieved by the three trained Spaniels.

A trained Springer steady to shot and wing and trained to work within gun range will *not* disturb new and unhunted territory ahead by chasing every hen pheasant that is flushed or every cock that is missed. It will be under perfect control and will be an *aid* to the gun rather than a hindrance.

The most common excuse given by the owner of an unsteady Springer which breaks shot and flush is that "he wants his dog to be there when the bird hits the ground in order not to lose the cripples". This is no argument at all and is really an excuse having no basis of fact. If permitted to acquire experience in hunting, any Spaniel gun dog with an average nose can learn to trail out and retrieve the crippled birds that fall before the gun, as well as those which try to avoid being flushed. The fact has been proved thousands of times in the hunting field and in field trials. It is the exception, rather than the rule, when an experienced Springer fails to produce a crippled running bird, even if he is held at the "hup" position for several minutes after the bird is downed.

To teach a dog to be steady, return to the yard and follow this procedure. First, stand in front of the dog and command him to "Hup!" and "Stay!". (Some trainers discontinue the use of the word "stay" at this stage of the training and rely on the word "hup" alone.) As the dog faces the trainer, the feathered retrieving buck should be tossed over the shoulder and the command "Stay!" or "Hup!" repeated several times. It may be necessary to make a quick grab for the dog to enforce the command "Stay!" because up to this time, he has been permitted to retrieve at will and may ignore the command to "Stay!". If the dog is restrained physically several times and scolded in a severe voice, he will usually revert to his earlier training and remain sitting as the buck is thrown over the trainer's shoulder. This lesson should be repeated several days in succession. If possible, the dog should never be permitted to retrieve if he leaves the sitting position without a command. Incidentally, the usual command for a retrieve is "Fetch!". At this stage the trainer usually couples the dog's name with the word "fetch", such as "Rover—fetch!". (Many trainers, especially those who follow field trials, gradually drop the word "fetch" and teach the dog to retrieve when only his name is called.)

After a day or two of standing in front of the dog to throw the buck, the trainer should then stand directly to one side of the dog, always being in such a position that he can provide the necessary restraint with his hands if the dog offers to make the retrieve without waiting for the command. This lesson should be repeated for several days until it is obvious that the dog has learned to wait for the command before retrieving. The trainer may then cnange position to a spot directly behind and throw the buck over the dog's head each time. In all likelihood, the

Miss Julia Meyers illustrating the correct method of teaching a Springer to be steady to flush and shot. Bonnie has been given the "hup" whistle command, and is waiting for the pigeon to be thrown.

After numerous lessons, Bonnie is permitted to flush a live pigeon. She is now ready to shot and will retrieve only on command.

Bonnie delivers the shot pigeon to hand after first assuming the "hup" (sit) position.

The training session is over and Bonnie demonstrates her good manners by walking easily at heel as trainer-owner Julia Meyers leaves the field.

Edward D. Porges with FTC Ludlovian Socks.
This great gun dog sired three English FTCs
and six more in the United States. His line
traces back to four of the six pivotal sources
mentioned by Sanderson elsewhere in this book.

Harold Jones, expert amateur trainer, accepts a retrieved pheasant from his
fine FTC Sir Cricket. Cricket and two of his kennelmates were handled by
Jones to the title.—*Photo, Bui.*

dog will remain steady most of the time, but when he does offer to break, the trainer must stop him by commanding "Hup!" in a loud voice. If this fails, the trainer must endeavor to run and pick up the buck before the dog does. Men over 40 may figure out an easier method, but younger men will find that the above practice not only amuses their neighbors, but also is wonderful exercise to reduce the waistline and improve the wind. Patience and practice will assure results. And never fail to pet the dog when he has performed properly, but be sure to withhold petting and verbal praise when he has failed to respond as desired.

The next step is to "hup" the dog in front of the trainer some ten yards, and toss the buck in the near-vicinity of the dog. Insist that no move to retrieve be made until the command is given. Gradually increase the distance between man and dog until it is possible to drop the dog thirty yards away and toss the buck practically under his nose while he remains steady. It is a good idea to walk out occasionally and retrieve the buck by hand in order to teach the dog that he cannot retrieve every time. After all, some birds will be missed and the dog must learn very early that he cannot retrieve every bird that is flushed.

Once the Spaniel has learned that he must not retrieve until ordered to do so in the yard, it is time to return to the field. First, cast the dog off to hunt (into the wind) and as he approaches from the left, the buck should be thrown to the extreme right. The trainer should step in front of the moving dog and give the whistle or the voice command to "Hup!". In all likelihood, the response will be good and the dog will drop after a step or two.

Repeat this procedure five times or so, and then let the dog hunt for a while uninterrupted. There should be another session of shorter duration before the trip afield is finished. The trainer should then go home and "help" his wife paint the storm windows before she gets the idea that being a "Spaniel widow" is worse than being a "Golf widow"!

The lesson described above should be repeated five or six times and then a dead pigeon should be substituted for the feather buck. The puppy will exhibit much more interest in the bird than in the buck and may attempt to break the first time or two. If the buck is always thrown as the prospect approaches, the trainer will be in position to step out *between* the dog and the bird, and thus will be able to enforce the command physically. Of course, the command "Hup!" or the whistle command to "hup" should be given each and every time and repeated several times if necessary.

When the dog is responding to this situation *every* time the trainer may substitute a clipped-wing, live pigeon for the dead bird. The dog will be more interested in the live bird than in the dead one and may attempt to break a time or two. Firmness and patience are still the proper attitudes, and no slackness is to be permitted. As the dog learns that he must obey the command with the live bird, the blank pistol should be reintroduced. The proper procedure is to fire the pistol, give the command "Hup!", and then toss the clipped-wing bird in a direction away from the dog. This may sound like something dreamed up by Rube Goldberg, but a little practice will soon enable the trainer to develop the proper coordination to perform all three actions simultaneously. It could be that the trainer will attempt to blow on the pigeon and throw the pistol on the first attempt. But such action will serve as a conversation piece at the office or as further evidence to the neighbors that Mr. Trainer is slightly "touched in the head".

One should be of firm resolve, however, for better days are coming. The freezer will be filled with fat cock pheasants and corn-fed mallards come November, and the trainer will receive twenty invitations to hunt with people with whom he had only a nodding acquaintance before he acquired the trained Springer Spaniel.

The next step is to kill some thrown flyers over the young dog as he sits at heel. It is wise to follow this procedure for 15 or 20 training sessions (50 to 100 pigeons) until the dog has become thoroughly conditioned to the fact that he must never retrieve until ordered to do so. It's a good idea to let him retrieve only four or five shot birds out of six. If the handler walks out and picks up an occasional bird while the dog remains sitting in his original position it will be helpful later on when two dogs are worked together while hunting or in a trial. (See picture which illustrates this technique.)

After the dog is responding well (perfectly) to the pistol and the thrown bird, the next and final step is to work on planted birds. The bird should be planted with its head facing down wind and the dog should be worked up to the bird on a cross wind (with the wind blowing against the right or the left side of his face instead of full into it). The trainer will have a better opportunity to step in front of the dog if he offers to break when the bird flushes. The whistle command to "hup" should be given at the exact instant the bird is flushed. If the dog has learned each step well, he will probably be steady on his first flushed pigeon. If he offers to break, the trainer (provided he has followed the plan outlined above) will be in a position to restrain the dog physically. It is well to have a friend along to do the actual shooting because the trainer will want to devote his full attention to the dog at this critical stage.

Enough progress has now been made so that one has only to repeat the foregoing procedure on every occasion possible. Most amateurs do their work in the field on the weekends. If the reader has any doubts about the success of weekend training, let him be assured that there are hundreds of sportsmen in the United States who do it successfully every year.

It is likely that there will be occasional lapses of memory on the dog's part as the training progresses. Low-flying birds or a bird shot too close may cause the pupil to break shot or flush. This is the time to "refresh" the dog's memory by running after him and carrying him back bodily to the point of flush. He should be placed firmly, and not too gently, on the ground in the sitting position, and chided in a rough tone of voice. A little repetition of the command "Hup, you so and so!" will usually do the trick.

There is one other method which may be used, but only as a last resort. This technique requires that a 40 or 50-foot nylon cord, called a check cord, be attached to the dog's collar and the command "Hup!" be enforced by a tight line as the bird is flushed. The check cord is believed by some to induce "pointing" in Spaniels if not properly used. The use of the check cord is not recommended to the hands of a novice trainer who might lack judgment as to its use. When all fails and it is decided, after mature reflection, that this is the only course left, the trainer must be as gentle with the dog as possible. Judicious use required that all slack be taken up on the line immediately at the instant of flush, and that the dog be held steady rather than jerked to a standstill. He should never be checked up while running at full speed. Rough treatment here may cause the Springer to become confused and develop into a blinker or pointer—both of which are serious faults.

Pointing game might seem a desirable trait to the novice Spaniel owner, but there are several good reasons why a Springer can never become a really satisfactory pointing dog. In the first place, a Springer Spaniel dog does not have the range, nose, or the stamina to hunt like a Pointer or an English Setter.

It is undoubtedly true that the early ancestors of the Springer and the English Setter were one and the same dog. It is also undoubtedly true that Springers (or at least certain strains of Springers) carry the genes for the pointing instinct. However, during the last hundred years in America, the English Setter and the Pointer have been developed into wide ranging, big-going dogs that can really "carry the mail" as far as quail dogs are concerned. They have no equals in this type of hunting. The Springer (the field strains), on the other hand, has been selected for its ability to work to the gun and to accept training kindly. No Springer can range with a top bird dog and no experienced dog man wants one that points, because it could never be more than a fifth-

Arthur Perle with his fine FTC
Alan-A-Dale   O'Glen   Robin
proudly pose with limit of Tule
Lake geese.

The veteran sportsman Tom Mofield and his
father with limit of Illinois geese retrieved by
a Springer gun dog that loved its work.—
Photo, Curtis.

rate pointing dog. Neither can good pointing dogs perform the functions of Spaniels.

A Springer cannot be developed into a satisfactory pointing dog for another reason, a reason which has to do with the Springer's nose. Through the last several hundred years, Spaniels have been bred for the type of nose that enables them to trail both fur and feathers and to locate game by body scent as well. Class pointing dogs rely strictly on body scent when it comes to finding game and have considerably less ability to trail moving game than do Spaniels. One cannot actually say that a Pointer or English Setter has a better nose than does a Spaniel, although they seem to be able to locate game by body scent from a greater distance than can a Spaniel. It is more accurate to say that the pointing dog's nose is better adapted to its specialized type of hunting, while the Spaniel's nose is more suitable for the work it is required to perform. It is the opinion of well-informed trainers, those who have had considerable experience with all three breeds, that each dog has a nose that is suited to its particular style of hunting and that even if it were possible to exchange the scenting apparatus, neither the pointing dogs nor the Spaniel could perform as well.

The last step in the intermediate training program for the Springer Spaniel is to make sure that "stopping to shot" is a firmly ingrained habit. During the earlier work it was suggested that every effort be made to have the dog in a sitting position when a pistol, and later a shotgun, was discharged. Some exceptionally bright Springer pupils are able to grasp the idea quickly from this early work and they become "steady to shot" after just a few training sessions. Even though this may occur, it is still sound training procedure, based on well-established principles of animal behavior, to devote some time to the specialized training which will make the dog letter-perfect in this department. One of the best places to give the special training for steadiness to shot is in the field with the blank pistol. To begin, cast the dog off with no planted birds and no wild birds, if possible. While the dog is quartering and responding to the whistle and to hand signals, fire the blank pistol. If the dog "hups"—wonderful. The only thing the trainer must do i to repeat the act eight or ten times and follow through with the same procedure for the next five or six trips to the field. If the dog does not stop and sit at the crack of the shot, the trainer immediately must give the verbal or whistle command to "hup".

During this phase of training, the blank pistol should be held high over the trainer's head. The act of firing the pistol, and giving the command "Hup!" by voice or whistle at the same time, will soon condition the dog to stop as he sees the trainer raise his arm overhead to discharge the pistol. This training procedure should be repeated at frequent intervals until the dog becomes thoroughly conditioned to "hupping" both to shot and to the trainer's upraised arm. On each occasion that the dog fails to respond, the trainer must rush out fast and scold the dog in a stern voice, accompanying the scolding with a shake of the collar if necessary. After the Spaniel's reflexes become thoroughly conditioned, he will be most dependable and reliable under normal circumstances.

The Springer puppy that was started in training some months ago is now an educated gun dog. He has finished "high school" and is ready for "college". Advanced training procedures will be described in the next chapter.

A Springer clearing a fence as he retrieves a live pheasant. Note the firm but soft grip by which this dog executes a perfect carry.

6
Advanced Field Training

THE PREVIOUS CHAPTERS on training have been concerned, primarily, with the man-made factors in the development of a fine gun dog. Up to this point, the emphasis has been on conditioning the dog to perform certain routine actions and to react in a desired manner to certain situations which give the trainer maximum control at all times. This portion of the education of a gun dog is most important because the dog's contribution to the function of filling the game bag is in direct proportion to the control which the handler can exercise in each and every situation which arises in the field.

Every experienced hunter knows that a wild, half-trained gun dog actually may be a hindrance in filling the game bag and providing a pleasant day afield, while a trained dog not only helps fill the bag, but is a joy to behold. Along with control, there are other attributes which a top gun dog must possess. These are natural ability and intense desire to hunt and find game, plus the experience to develop these instinctive traits. This chapter will be devoted to a discussion of these factors, which are of equal if not greater importance than control.

One of the more amusing aspects of the history of hunting which appears regularly in the works of authors both modern and ancient, is the frequent reference to the fact that game is in much shorter supply than it was in *their* father's day. In fact, one writer of the Middle Ages was so worked up over the fact, that he doubted that it was worthwhile to train or keep a hunting dog. If all the gloomy forecasts about the prevalence of upland game and waterfowl were true, all species of same would be as extinct as the mythical dodo bird and there would not be

Louis Bui teaches his young Springer gun dog to hold a pheasant just retrieved from a California rice stubble.—*Photo, Bui.*

The veteran California sportsman, Orm Bequette, with his home-trained Springer, Orm's Emissary. Bequette handled this fine young male to an Amateur as well as an Open Field Championship.

any purpose in this book or any of the others which appear each year on dogs, hunting, shooting, and related subjects.

The author does not want to break the pattern of gloom about the decreasing game supply which has been the hallmark of all writers on the subject for the past five hundred years. Therefore, the statement that it is difficult to give a gun dog the proper experience on game follows in the well-established pattern of those "who have trod these sacred halls before". The fact remains, however, that in these days of intensive cultivation of farm land and two automobiles in every farmer's garage, it is not always possible to put a young gun dog on wild game as frequently as one would like, because the fence corners are plowed and the marginal land is utilized for grazing and other agrarian endeavors. Therefore, the contemporary trainer of a gun dog will have to be alert to all possibilities for giving his dog the opportunity to develop the instinctive urge to hunt.

Every dog in general, and every Spaniel in particular, has some natural ability to hunt and to find game. It is up to the trainer to give the dog the experience necessary to develop fully whatever natural ability he may possess. The old adage that "practice makes perfect" is a truism when applied to a gun dog. The trainer, then, should take every opportunity to expose the dog to game and to do it as frequently as possible.

Students of the outdoors know that most species of game birds and animals usually follow a regular, clock-like pattern of action. An old hen pheasant will take her brood of chicks off the roost at about the same hour each day. They will feed and go to water and follow a most rigid schedule. The trainer of a gun dog will do well to work his dog in the field as early in the morning as possible or just before dark in the evening. The birds will sit more tightly at this time and the young dog will be able to find and flush them with greater ease.

A good routine to follow with a dog at this stage is to go to a field where game is known to abide. The dog should be "hupped" and then ordered to hunt (into the wind). When he strikes scent, the dog will usually indicate the freshness of the scent by his actions. On a day when scent lies well and the dog "makes game" strongly, he should be allowed to follow the line and come up with the bird or rabbit, if possible. The dog will usually trail faster than the handler can walk and may soon be out of normal gun range. When he gets to the limits, the handler should blow the stop whistle and insist that the dog respond by "hupping". The handler should walk up, pet the dog, and then order him to resume trailing. Young dogs will be momentarily confused and may experience some difficulty in again picking up the line of scent. If the handler remains perfectly still and lets the dog work it out, more often than not the dog will again pick up the line of scent and return to trailing.

The dog should be required to "hup" each time he gets out of normal gun range and never ordered to resume hunting until the handler arrives. Repeated efforts along these lines will increase the dog's ability to trail and will teach the handler much that he did not know before about both dog and game. If the dog is trailing a pheasant, he should be required to honor the flush and to remain seated for five or ten seconds. It is much better, of course, to shoot game over the dog every time he flushes. But this is not possible except during the open season or when using planted birds, so the next best thing is to let the dog learn to flush and hunt without shooting.

After the bird has flushed and the dog has honored the flush by sitting, he should be called in to heel, petted, and made over, and then cast off in the opposite direction from the flight of the bird. Young prospects will want to chase, but repetitious use of a firm "No!" and insistent whistle signals will serve to prevent a chase or bolt in the direction of the flushed bird. After the young dog has become proficient in following the lines of scent left by rabbits and bird, the trainer should occasionally cast the dog off the line and require him to hunt in another direction without flushing the bird or rabbit. The young pupil may be most reluctant to leave the line, but the handler must be firm and insistent, which will serve to increase the handler's control. This has a practical side, too, as no hunter wants his dog to follow game into a restricted area where hunting may not be permitted or to cross a highway in pursuit of game.

A word of caution is in order here in regard to the manner in which the dog is permitted to work, for the author recognizes fully the dangers of working up game which is not shot. If not properly controlled, a young dog may cease to mark or may develop into a low-headed rabbit dog with his nose glued to the ground and with little interest in anything else. These pitfalls may be avoided by never permitting the dog to potter or linger (smell around in one place) on stale scent. The novice trainer will soon be able to distinguish between stale scent and fresh scent, and so will the dog. If the young dog does not attempt to move out on the scent, he should be called off by whistle or voice, cast in another direction, and kept moving. A dog should *never* be allowed to potter. He should be kept moving and hunting; this will be no problem if the dog has been trained properly on the whistle. The trainer should, if necessary, enforce his command by a firm shake of the dog's collar or some well-chosen words suitable to the occasion. The dog must be kept moving and quartering in the desired pattern (similar to that of a windshield wiper on a car).

The answer to those who do not believe in permitting a young dog to work wild game which cannot be shot, lies in the fact that thousands upon thousands of hunting dogs have been trained this way down through the ages. Until the recent adoption by the pointing dog people of the use of planted game, nearly 100 percent of pointing dogs in the United States were trained almost entirely on wild game which was not shot for them. If one keeps the Spaniel moving and shoots a few pigeons over him each week, there will be little loss of marking ability and no encouragement to potter, *even if worked almost daily* on wild birds. This is no theory—it has been tested by actual experience on many thousands of dogs.

The trainer may have some difficulty in keeping the dog steady to flush on rabbits or other ground game at this period. If so, a little specialized yard work may be given. This is accomplished by taking the skin (or pelt) of a rabbit and fixing it to a croquet ball, with the hair on the outside. This simulated rabbit can then be concealed in the trainer's coat and rolled rapidly on the ground in front of the Spaniel as he hunts. Much repetition will develop the dog's steadiness to rabbits. The basis of the training principle behind this trick is in keeping with well-established laws of animal behavior. If this act is repeated, and is accompanied each time by the stop or "hup" signal of the whistle or voice, the dog will have his reflexes conditioned so thoroughly that he will soon begin to drop to the simulated rabbit flush automatically.

It may be necessary to "refresh" the dog's memory by the use of stern words and a little shaking up at first, but once the idea is understood, the battle is practically won. When the dog has firmly fixed in mind the habit of stopping on the rolling ball with rabbit pelt, and is doing it automatically without a command of voice or whistle, it is a simple matter to substitute real rabbits for the ball and require the dog to stop at each flush.

In the early chapters on training, it was suggested that the command to "hup" be accompanied by the raising of the hand. During the advanced work in the field, further conditioning to this arm command should be given. At every working session, the dog should be required to stop and "hup" on the silent command of the upraised arm. It should be given, of course, when the dog is glancing at the handler. At first it may be necessary to accompany the hand signal with one blast of the whistle. Later, as the pupil progresses, the whistle may be eliminated and the dog required to "hup" each time the hand is raised. This may serve a useful purpose if the dog is upwind from the handler on the windy day when the voice and whistle may not be heard. It will also prove most useful in the city if the dog attempts to cross from the opposite side of the street in front of an approaching automobile. It will serve a useful purpose on many occasions in the field, too, when the handler may observe game which he does not wish to disturb by a vocal command.

The dog should be encouraged to take directions while hunting or retrieving by being sent in a definite direction each time he is cast off to hunt. The handler should always point in the direction in which he wishes the dog to hunt. If the dog is slow to respond, a step or two taken in the desired direction will encourage the prospect to work toward that general area. Repeated efforts of this sort will produce the desired results. Many hunters who know the habits of game have trained their dogs to respond almost entirely to hand signals and have had excellent results. Certainly one in woodcock or grouse cover will not wish to arouse the entire countryside and disturb the game unduly by constant voice and whistle signals. The average Spaniel, and even those below average, have the ability to learn to take direction by hand.

Hand Signals to "Come In"

Another most useful response which all polished gun dogs should learn is to come to heel when a hand signal is given. There are several positions of the hands which may be used for this signal. But one which gun dogs seem to grasp readily is to hold the hands down to the side but slightly away from the body, with the palms out and the fingers spread. If a dog has been taught to respond to this silent command, it will enable the handler to bring the dog to heel in a strong wind when the voice or whistle signal might not be heard, or when two dogs are working and the handler wishes to call one in while the other hunts or retrieves.

Thirty minutes of yard work in which the dog is "hupped" and given the verbal or whistle command to come in simultaneously with the outspread hand signal is usually enough to get the idea over to the pupil. Additional work on this signal should be given in the field from time to time. For instance, when one has worked up a couple of pigeons and is returning to the automobile, the dog can be "hupped" as the trainer walks away. When the distance between man and dog is approximately 35 yards, the trainer may stop and give the voice and hand signal to come in to heel. After a few lessons, the voice command can be eliminated and only the hand signal given. The dog will soon learn to respond and if the response is not perfect, he can be encouraged by voice or whistle.

The trainer must always insist on immediate response to this command, as well as all other commands. The dog can be shaken up slightly if he fails to respond with alacrity and should be rewarded *every* time that he obeys. The reward should be in the form of a kind word or a friendly pat.

It is never a good idea to call a dog to heel merely to pet him. This may establish a habit pattern in which the dog is constantly checking in to the handler. Most dogs soon learn to know when they have pleased their handler and most Springers, especially those of field breeding, have a strong desire to please. The dog should always be rewarded by voice.

The ideal gun dog is one that quarters his ground almost mechanically in training and learns to know his range. This means that he knows about how far on each side of the handler he is to cast and will turn automatically without a whistle or voice command. When a dog does this automatically, it is said that he "knows his range". This is a most valuable trait and the trainer who wants a really polished dog should make concerted efforts toward this goal. It has a practical purpose, too, in that constant whistling and yelling will disturb game in the field and is most annoying to friends who may be hunting with the dog's owner. Overhandling indicates that the Springer is only half trained.

The trainer should, first of all, know his dog and how he works. Second, he must learn to develop confidence in his dog. If a handler sees that his dog is at the limits of his range (to the side) and there is a likely spot of cover 15 feet beyond the spot at which the dog would normally turn, it is well for the handler to refrain from blowing the turn whistle because the dog probably should work the small spot of cover. The wise handler will let the dog go another few feet to check the likely looking spot and will take a few steps in that direction, in the event the dog pushes a bird or rabbit from the spot. A good, experienced dog should demonstrate some "game sense", and working out a spot of likely looking cover or continuing down a fence line for a few yards is one indication that game sense is developing.

It is well to trust a dog in these circumstances, or many others of a similar nature, because most dogs can find more game accidentally than any human can find on purpose. One should always trust the dog's nose. If he indicates game, no matter how sparse the cover may be or how unlikely it appears as a logical place for game, the wise hunter will always trust the dog. Occasionally the dog will be wrong, but he will be right more times than he is wrong if he has an average nose and has learned to use it.

There are many occasions when it appears that a Springer is wrong and that he has become completely befuddled about a bird, especially a crippled running pheasant. At one of the National championship field trials for Springers a few years ago, a cock pheasant was shot over one of the dogs. In full view of the handler, the judges, and the gallery, it appeared to run rapidly in the same direction it was flying when shot. The handler sent his dog to make the retrieve, which is always very sporting. The dog went to the "fall" (spot where the bird struck the ground) and trailed it in the direction in which everyone thought the bird had gone. After a few seconds, the dog (apparently still trailing) turned and headed back toward the handler, who attempted to stop the dog and send him in the opposite direction. He responded as ordered but would hunt out for a few yards, then reverse his direction and head back toward the handler. After the third time, the handler gave up and let the dog have his head. Imagine this man's surprise when the dog picked up and retrieved the cock which had attempted to hide virtually at the judge's feet. Unfortunately, this sort of thing happens to everyone who trains dogs, and will continue to happen in the future. Put as much trust in the dog as possible and always remember that the dog's nose, while not infallible, is more likely to be right than wrong.

There are a good many times during the shooting year when a situation arises where game is very abundant and the anxious hunter will have a fast and furious few minutes of shooting, with several birds down. If this occurs in a duck blind, or a hot mourning-dove stand, the dog should be kept at heel during the few minutes of fast shooting and not sent to retrieve until several birds are on the ground.

According to Clifford H. Wallace, one of the leading Spaniel and Retriever professional trainers, it is improbable that most dogs can mark and *remember* accurately the fall of more than three birds. Even this feat of marking and remembering requires considerable experience. It would seem, therefore, that teaching a gun dog to accept help in situations of this sort would be almost a "must" for serious hunters. There are also numerous occasions when a lightly shot bird will fly over a hill or beyond some trees and then change direction when out of the dog's line of vision. All retrieves of this sort can be handled much faster and with little or no wasted time if the trainer is willing to spend a little time teaching the dog to take directions.

A young Spaniel can be started on this phase of his education by the use of two retrieving bucks (double retrieves). A very young dog has a short span of attention, and even though one throws two bucks for a five-months-old puppy, he will probably forget about the second by the time he has brought in the first. Nevertheless, the puppy should be started on double retrieves at a very young age. It will be necessary for the trainer to walk out a few times to the second one while repeating the command "Get back!" and making, at the same time, a throwing motion with the arm. After several sessions of ten minutes duration, the young prospect will soon catch on that there is something for him to retrieve when he hears the "Get back!" command and observes the throwing motion of the trainer's arm.

As the dog learns to handle double retrieves, both of which are in about the same location, the handler can begin to toss the bucks farther and farther apart, until after two or three weeks, the throws are made in exactly opposite directions. To make the work a little more difficult, one of the bucks can be thrown while the dog is retrieving the first one. When this is done, the handler should always give the dog the direction of the second fall by pointing his arm on a plane level with the dog's head in the direction of the fall which the dog did not see. The command "Fetch!" or "Get back!" should be given at the same time. If this practice is repeated at regular intervals, the young dog soon learns to attempt a retrieve even though he has not seen any object fall. When he will do this, he is well on his way to becoming a good blind retriever.

As the dog attempts these blind retrieves, he will not always be able to find the buck immediately because of wind direction and faulty memory. A dog may be within three feet of a buck, or even a live bird, and not be able to scent it if the wind is blowing from the dog to the buck or bird. This is the reason experienced dogs will sometimes cast out in circles when searching for a shot bird. They are using the wind and have learned by trial and error that the bird may be found if they circle around and take the wind just right. This is the time to get the idea over to the dog that he can get help from the handler. The dog should be allowed to search for the unmarked buck and then his attention should be attracted by voice or whistle; the handler should then wave his arm in the direction of the fall. Repeated practice will teach the dog that he can look to the handler for help.

As the dog gets older and more experienced, it is best to give him the stop whistle, and after he has "hupped", to indicate the location of the bird with a wave of the hand. When the dog is taking directions nicely, the job is completed. Brushing up will be required from time to time and the trainer should devote five minutes to blind retrieves in the field at the conclusion of each session of bird work and shooting.

It has been proven repeatedly in the animal behavior clinics that a dog's vision is more acute on moving objects than on stationary ones.

If the dog marks the fall short, the command "Get back!" should be given and a throwing motion with the arm repeated simultaneously. Persistent effort will teach the dog to respond by hunting out farther, or to the right or left, as the case may be. When the dog is going out willingly to make cold, blind retrieves (looking for a bird he did not see and without a shot from the gun), he is approaching that degree of perfection that entitles him to be described as a good blind retriever. This is a most useful attribute in hunting and one that a really polished dog should have.

One word of caution is necessary, however. All work on blind retrieving should be done in moderation and intermixed with practice in "marked" retrieving. If too much work is given on blind retrieving, it may cause some dogs to lose interest in marking and depend too much on the trainer's help in locating the bird. When this condition develops, it is said that the dog is "overtrained". A good gun dog will always show initiative and persistence at the fall of a shot bird. He should work until the handler stops him to give directions. If the dog searches for a minute or two, and then stops of his own volition and looks to the handler for help, the blind retrieving work should be discontinued for a month or two and the dog permitted to retrieve only marked falls. No help should be given to a dog while he is acting in this manner.

One way to start a dog on blind retrieves, if he was not given the work on doubles in the early stages, is to drop a dead bird behind the handler in full view of the dog (which is walking at heel). When the handler is a few yards away and down wind from the bird, the dog may be commanded to fetch, and throwing motions may be made with the arm in the direction of the bird. As the dog learns to go back a few yards and pick up the dead bird, the distance may be increased a few yards until the dog is going back as far as 50 yards for a bird which he did not see the trainer drop. Some dogs will learn to follow directly to the fall, the line of scent left by the trainer. When this occurs, the trainer should take pains to toss the bird a considerable distance to the right or left of his foot scent so the dog will have to search for it and not just follow the handler's foot scent back to the fall.

Placing dead birds or the buck in cover while the dog is concealed or otherwise unable to watch, is another way to start blind retrieving. One can also secure the help of a friend to plant dead birds or the buck in this phase of the training routine.

By the time he has learned all, or nearly all, of the actions described in the various chapters on education of the gun dog, the average Springer Spaniel will be approaching two years of age. If these various lessons have been well learned, the owner has a beautifully trained,

Cecil Gipson and FTC Shooters Lucky Headliner after a successful Western pheasant hunt.

Sam Inkley and his two fine gun dogs with the evidence to prove again that Springers are great pheasant dogs.

polished, experienced gun dog which will provide many hours of pleasant recreation in the field. Both man and dog will be healthier and happier for the time spent in the outdoors and can look forward to eight or more years of good hunting together. If the trainer has devoted the time required to teach the dog everything suggested, it is quite likely that he will have joined a field trial club so that he will have an additional motive for spending more time afield with his dog. Most field trial enthusiasts shoot over their Spaniels for forty or more weeks each year, and it is debatable whether they derive more pleasure from field trials and hunting, or in the weekly training sessions with their friends. Real dyed-in-the-wool fans say it is the greatest sport in the world and will back this statement with money or action. The author is quite prone to admit that, after 40 years of such activity, he has found no reason to disagree with the above opinion.

In conclusion, it should be said that no two dogs ever respond to training in exactly the same way. It is, therefore, impossible to prescribe a training method that will fit each dog perfectly. The language barrier, which prevails among all humans, makes it impossible to explain in exact detail every individual act which the trainer must perform. It is assumed that the person interested enough to follow the routines and suggestions reported here will understand this fact. Any training routine should be mixed with an equal part of common sense, and the trainer must *always* be sure that the dog enjoys the work.

The major requirement of a good trainer is the ability to teach the dog to *respect* the trainer rather than to fear him. The various training exercises suggested are designed to promote this condition. By applying extreme force, anyone can force any dog to "hup" in five minutes. It takes much longer to *train* a dog to "hup" or to perform any other action. But the end results are much better by training than by forcing.

One should never lose sight of the fact that for every unit of force applied to a dog, there will be an equal unit of reaction. If, for example, a dog is beaten and forced to retrieve, the reaction may show up in the manner of flushing game. Dogs beaten to force steadiness may become blinkers. Dogs beaten or forced to turn on the whistle may become bolters. Thus, training, and not forcing, is the desirable method.

Some trainers who use extreme force do produce an occasional good dog, but for every good specimen they turn out, they ruin ten.

There is never an occasion when a dog should be beaten or abused. The trainer who thinks so is 50 years behind the times. One should keep this fact in mind at all times and never, never abuse a gun dog.

It is wrong from the standpoint of the well-established natural laws of animal behavior and from the standpoint of acceptable human behavior. This principle was learned by actual experience and has had a good deal of thoughtful consideration and study. It is hoped that this suggestion, above all others, will be followed. It is the single greatest training aid in this book.

The famous movie star, Robert Montgomery, was a top wing shot, and was frequently invited to shoot at field trials where he was not judging or handling his own Springer.

Diablos Ligero Skipper demonstrates a valuable training tool—the water retrieving buck. Skipper is owned and was trained and handled to his field championship by Mrs. Dorothy Alvestad.—*Photo, Bui.*

7
Water Work

O<small>NE</small> OF the most useful functions a Springer Spaniel can perform is to retrieve dead and wounded game from water. The dog's expert performance of this function will pay for his keep many times over, so the wise sportsman will make every effort to provide the necessary training and experience which make for good water retrieving.

If one wishes a really top duck dog, one of the Retriever breeds, particularly the Labrador Retriever, is the specialist at this work. The Retrievers have the required coat (two of them, in fact) and can stand the tough, grueling conditions that prevail in retrieving ducks and other waterfowl from icy water in freezing temperatures. However, the average United States sportsman, who can get in only a half-dozen days of duck shooting each year, will find the properly trained Springer an excellent water retriever as well as a top upland game dog.

The prospect's initial introduction to water is all important. Here is a good procedure to follow:

After the puppy is six or eight months old and is retrieving nicely from land, he should be taken for his introduction to water to a nearby pond or lake with gently sloping banks. The trainer should be equipped with waders or a bathing suit, for it will probably be necessary for him to enter the water. A nice warm sunny day in the late spring or early summer should be chosen for the comfort of both dog and man.

A boat bumper or canvas retrieving buck should be taken along, and a blank pistol, too; water work should not be started until the dog has been shot over in the field.

At first, let the puppy ramble about the banks of the lake for a short period of time, say five minutes, until he feels at home and has investigated all the strange new scents.

After the puppy has become acclimated and adjusted to this new terrain, the trainer should call him and walk out a few feet into the water. There is a good possibility that the dog will follow and frisk around playfully in the water. If he does, he should be allowed to play and dash in and out of the water to his heart's content. If the trainer remains in water up to a depth of about six or eight inches, the dog will, too, although he may dash in and out in a playful mood.

If the dog attempts to swim, so much the better. If he makes no effort to swim, the trainer should walk out a few feet until he is in water approximately up to his knees. If the dog does not follow, he should be coaxed (not forced) to venture out this far. If he swims and wades to the trainer, he should be petted and made over as a reward for the effort.

Many young Spaniels have an instinctive liking for water and will start to swim immediately. Their first efforts are usually quite clumsy and they will splash a good deal with their front feet, which they attempt to lift out of the water with each stroke. Some encouragement by voice and petting will help build confidence and many of them enjoy the swimming from the very first experience.

If, however, the young dog exhibits any fear of water, it will be necessary to build up his confidence by making repeated trips to the pond and by letting the dog become adjusted by repeatedly coaxing him to enter as the trainer wades close to the shore. If the trainer is patient, even the most backward pupil will respond eventually to kind treatment and encouragement.

Once the dog appears to have overcome his first mild fear or uncertainty, a short retrieve should be tried in the shallow water where it is not necessary for the dog to swim. This may be on the first trip, or the fifth, depending on the pupil's response to the new experience.

When first sent to retrieve from water, the puppy should be started from the position at heel and very close to the water's edge on a gently sloping shoreline. The buck should be thrown only three or four feet and never into deep water. Because the puppy has been retrieving the buck at home in the yard, he will know immediately what is expected. It is entirely possible that the dog will dash into the water, seize the buck and deliver it to hand. If he does so, he should be praised and rewarded by voice or petting.

The retrieve should be repeated five or six times in very shallow water. Then the distance should be increased gradually, so that the puppy will have to swim a few strokes to reach the buck. After three or four successful retrieves at this distance, the lesson should be stopped for the day. It is always important to quit while the dog is still enthusiastic and enjoying the work. The trainer should then put on his walking shoes and take the dog for a brisk run in cover for some ten minutes to dry off. And it is always a good idea to check the dog's ears to insure that they are dry, for it is possible that the excess splashing resulting from dashing about in shallow water and from clumsy attempts to swim may have caused considerable water to enter the ears. Ears that are damp inside make ideal breeding places for fungus and infection which can cause trouble later. A towel or handkerchief may be used to dry out the inside of the ears if they appear wet. Do not rub—blot up the water.

The trips to the pond should be repeated at frequent intervals and the length of the retrieves gradually extended until the puppy is swimming out 30 or 40 yards. The young dog should, of course, be required to sit at heel and await the command to retrieve each time the buck is thrown. After the first two or three lessons, the dog's swimming will improve and there will be considerably less splashing with the front feet.

After the dog has learned to like the water, the blank pistol should also be used each time the dog retrieves, until an association between the sound of the shot and the thrown buck is well established. The proper sequence of action is to fire the pistol and *then* throw the buck. It is assumed, of course, that the dog has been shot over, or at least has heard the pistol discharged on land a number of times before he has taken to water.

As the dog gains confidence and is completing 40 yard retrieves with ease, the trainer should enlist the aid of a friend as he proceeds to the next phase of the training. The next step is to have the friend place himself on a point of land, or on a boat, raft, or island, 40 or 50 yards away but in full view of the dog. The friend should then fire the pistol and throw the buck high in the air, at a distance not greater than 40 yards from the dog. At the command to retrieve, the young prospect should enter the water briskly, swim out, retrieve the buck, and deliver it carefully to the trainer's hand. If the dog attempts to do anything other than to return to the trainer, a few calls on the whistle should lead him to do as he should. The distance of the retrieves can gradually be increased until the young dog is swimming 100 yards or more each time.

No lesson, however, should be extended so long that the dog appears to be getting bored or tired. It is always wise to stop while he is still keen and fresh, and never work the prospect until he tires. If trips are made repeatedly during the summer, the young dog will become an expert swimmer and will learn to love the water.

In the early water work, the trainer should stand close to the water's edge in order to take the buck from the young Spaniel, before he has a chance to put it down. Most young dogs will drop the buck immediately after they are clear of the water in order to shake the water from their coats. If the trainer stands close to the shoreline during the early lessons and accepts delivery of the buck before the dog is entirely clear of the water, it will be helpful. The distance which the trainer stands from the water's edge can be increased gradually until he is back some 10 or 15 feet.

By repeated urging and coaxing, the dog eventually can be taught to hold the buck until it is safely delivered to the trainer's hands. All dogs instinctively want to shake to remove water from their coats. With patience and plenty of encouragement, they can be trained to delay the shaking action *until after* they deliver. When the dog attempts to drop the buck to shake, the trainer can help eliminate the fault if he will run back from the water a few yards, as if he were going to leave the area. At the same time, he should warn the dog repeatedly to "Hold it!". This will help overcome the vice and will speed up the return. Every effort should be made to instill the idea in the dog's mind that he *must* deliver before shaking. If the habit of shaking before delivering the object becomes fixed, it is difficult to overcome.

There is a good practical reason for insisting on immediate delivery of the buck. If a hunting dog is sent to retrieve a crippled duck or goose, the cripple may run if it is placed on the ground while the dog stops to shake. In such cases, the cripple may take cover in the nearest patch of cattails. A keen Spaniel will, of course, go after the bird and, if it is a strong runner, there may be a time lapse of 10 or 15 minutes as the dog relocates and retrieves the bird. This is wasted time, for while the dog is chasing a cripple up and down the bank or in the water, no ducks or geese will come in to work the blocks.

A good water retriever must be taught to work through blocks or decoys without becoming tangled in the anchor lines. This phase of the Spaniel's education is accomplished by starting the dog (after he is well adjusted to the water) to retrieve a dead pigeon, pheasant, or duck.

After the Springer is handling the dead bird properly and appears to like the work, one decoy should be planted on *the shore* and the dog permitted to investigate it thoroughly. After he has sniffed and checked it over, the dog should be called to heel and sent to retrieve

Oregon sportsman Paul Diegel prepares to give FTC Mahogany Kit and trial winner Sunny Weather of Silver Creek a workout in water retrieving. This is an excellent way to keep gun dogs in condition during hot summer weather.— *Photo, Dittebrandt.*

FTC Timpanagos Papaya retrieving a mallard duck to James R. Dodson.

a thrown dead bird, so that it is necessary to pass to one side of the decoy. After a few retrieves near the land-locked decoy, it should be moved a few feet into the water, and the dead bird thrown in such a way that the dog has to pass the decoy to reach the bird. If the dog attempts to molest or retrieve the decoy, he should be scolded and told in no uncertain manner (with stern use of the word "No!"), that he is to leave it strictly alone.

A few retrieves to one side of the floating decoy are usually enough to get the idea over to the dog that he is to ignore the wooden duck and retrieve only the dead one. The trainer can then gradually increase the number of decoys to two, three, four, five, etc., but they should be placed in very shallow water and the dog always sent to retrieve to one side of the setup. The direction of the retrieves should be changed gradually until the bird or buck is thrown directly over the decoys. If the dog attempts to swim through them to reach the thrown bird, he can be warned away, by sternly repeating the word "No!".

If he persists in swimming through the middle of the decoys (they should be bunched in a small area at first), he eventually will become fouled in the anchor lines, and probably will complete a few retrieves with one or more decoys dragging behind. The stern use of the word "No!" will eventually teach the dog to give the setup a wide berth, especially after he has become fouled a few times. Getting the idea over is just a matter of patience and persistence on the part of the trainer. The application of good common sense, and the gradual introduction of each new step, will work wonders and produce excellent results with any normal Springer.

When this lesson has been mastered, the decoys can be moved further out in the lake and spread to simulate a regular setup in a duck marsh. The dead pigeon or bird can then be thrown from the island or boat and the dog sent to retrieve from the mainland with a big spread of decoys between the dog and the thrown bird. If given lots of water work, the dog will learn eventually to handle the situation. And when he does, this phase of the training is completed.

All that remains is to teach the dog to work from a blind and a boat, and to pick up a live duck. This can be done by building a small brush blind with a small hole on one side, adjacent to the spot where the dog is *always* required to sit. A few birds thrown after the blank pistol has been discharged, or a few live pigeons shot from a boat or island, soon will condition the dog to sit in the blind in the proper position to observe the proceedings and to mark the fall of the birds. He should be required to sit in one place from 10 to 15 minutes at a time, and the trainer's assistant instructed to throw the bird and fire the pistol after such a length of time has elapsed. The dog soon will learn to watch for the falling bird every time he hears the shot and eventually will be a good marker from a blind.

Training a dog to work from a boat is a relatively simple matter if it is not attempted until he has learned to retrieve from water. He should be taken for a short boat ride and required to sit in one spot in the boat. After the young prospect has been in a boat two or three times and is no longer nervous (he may be, the first time or two) a clipped-wing pigeon should be thrown from the boat while the boat is beached. The dog should then be urged to retrieve from the land-locked craft.

When he returns with the bird, the dog should be urged to enter the boat to make the delivery. Naturally, one should use a flat bottom craft with as little free board as possible. One should not attempt to work the dog from a canoe, unless he is an expert seaman and the canoe is a very beamy, stable craft. It is assumed that if this type of training is given to the dog, all duck shooting will be done from a very stable craft, one that a wet, 50-pound Springer could not capsize.

When the dog has acquired the knack of retrieving in and out of the beached or land-locked craft, it should be moved out into shallow water and the performance repeated. If the water is just deep enough to float the craft, the dog will be able to climb in after his retrieve and deliver to hand.

After the dog is working well from the boat in shallow water, the boat can be moved out to a depth of three or four feet and the performance repeated. When the dog returns to the boat with the bird, it should be taken from him while he is still in the water, and then he should be encouraged to climb into the boat. It will be necessary to coax him a good deal at first, and perhaps to render some aid by a pull on his back or the ruff of the neck. He should be rewarded by voice and petting every time he gets in the boat either with, or without, the help of the trainer. Many Springers can develop the knack of climbing into a boat with low free board by hooking their front feet over the gunwale and pumping their back feet. Some never acquire the knack and will always require some human aid to perform the act. In any event, it is a great help to have a dog that will enter the water from a boat to retrieve, even if he does require some help to get back in.

It is most important and cannot be overemphasized that one should never force or throw a dog into the water from a boat. (Any dog of any breed can be taught to swim and love water if the trainer is patient and makes the lessons easy and short.) Also, a new lesson should never be attempted until the previous one has been learned carefully. One must *never* forget that a dog must not be forced to do anything. He

FTC Ludlovian Tiny of Hardthill completing a tough retrieve. Her owner, Lee Caya, is a fine trainer as well as a trial judge of Spaniels and Pointers.— *Photo, Shafer.*

should be trained, and he should be rewarded with a pat or a kind word for all of his successful actions *every time* he performs them. Experienced trainers develop this habit until it becomes an unconscious action on their part every time. Developing the habit will pay many dividends.

Most dogs want to please their masters. If one makes a game of all the lessons, especially in the early stages, the Springer soon will learn to look forward to the training sessions. Once an action becomes a habit, the dog can be depended upon to perform as desired. This applies to both land and water work and the wise trainer will never forget it.

Some dogs that have had a bad fright at the water never recover from it. In such cases, force training is the answer, but only as a last resort. It should *never* be attempted by the novice, and is properly employed only by a good professional or experienced amateur. Results of force training in the water or on the land are not always uniformly good. It is a risky business and should be employed only as a last resort.

Regardless of the breed, every good duck dog that is worthy of the name must learn to take directions and to complete blind retrieves on land and in the water. The reason is obvious to any duck hunter and will not be discussed here. But the technique for teaching a gun dog this most worthwhile and useful function should be started in the early training, as suggested elsewhere in the chapters on training.

If the dog has learned to perform on land as suggested previously, it is relatively simple to teach him to do the same thing in water. Most dogs that will take hand signals on land, will do so in water if given a little work. In this case, the trainer should always precede any hand signals given in the water by the "hup", or stop, whistle command. Naturally a Spaniel cannot "hup" or sit in deep water and the "hup" whistle command, in this case, is given merely to get the dog's attention. Once he looks back at the handler, the proper signal may be given to send the dog to the right or to the left or farther out. This latter command should always be accompanied by the voice command "Get back!".

If the dog does not catch on to the hand signals in water, the handler may speed up the learning process by tossing a small stone in the desired direction as he waves the dog to the right or left or orders him to go farther out. This practice is usually not necessary, except in extreme cases, and should be discontinued after a few sessions in order that the dog will not grow to expect the stone-tossing act each time he is sent for a blind retrieve in the water.

Blind retrieves and other difficult types of retrieves are taught in great detail to all of the Retriever breeds. They perform to perfection and all laymen and gun dog people are constantly amazed at the skill they demonstrate both in land and water work. Spaniels can learn to perform equally well, and do so every day, but usually not with the finish and polish that is required of a high class Retriever gun dog.

If each step has been followed as suggested, and the young dog has not been started on a new lesson before the earlier one was mastered from water, blind, or boat, through decoys and in open or marshy water, he should now be a good retriever. It only remains now to try out the dog's new skills and to develop them fully by shooting lots of fat mallards over him. One should keep one eye on the dog on the first few hunting trips, and correct at once any slackness which deviates— evenly slightly—from the routine learned in the summer training. From much hunting experience with wild birds, the dog will learn to hunt for cripples on the banks of rivers and streams, and to work out the cattails and wild rice beds when a strong cripple attempts to hide. He will also learn to pursue, and eventually capture, a diving cripple. And when he has successfully done so, there won't be enough money in America to buy him.

As a final step in the water training procedure, a few domestic mallards should be procured from a farmer or a poultry market. The dog should first retrieve a dead duck from land a few times and then try it from water. If the results are good, the dog may go on to the next phase of the procedure. The legs and the wings of one of the ducks should be shackled with a light cord. The duck should then be tossed into the water and the dog permitted to retrieve it alive a few times. He will need this experience to enable him to handle cripples during the shooting season. If the trainer was fortunate enough to get a diving duck, it will teach the dog much about this type of behavior which wing tipped mallard sometimes exhibit.

In any event, if the dog handles the live ducks in good fashion, the one remaining requirement is a blustery, windy day when the duck season opens. Such a day will guarantee that both trainer and the dog will have themselves a ball.

If the shooting is good, two or three trips to the trainer's favorite duck marsh will finish out the dog's education to this type of shooting. If the ducks are not working, the trainer can call a few crows to test his shooting eye and the dog's retrieving ability. In any event, he now has a trained duck dog.

FTC Busy Bruning of Ashaba, owned, trained and handled by the late A. P. Moecher (see page 26). Busy was the second Springer to earn the title in the West.

8

Training Procedures
To Correct Faults

THERE are any number of faults which Springer gun dogs may display. A few of the more common ones will be discussed in this chapter. But before considering them, keep foremost in mind that it is much simpler to train a dog properly in the first place than it is to correct a fault. The evidence to support this fact was revealed several years ago by the animal research people at Cornell University. In their studies, they learned that the old adage, "You can't teach an old dog new tricks", was not true. You *can* teach an old dog new tricks (correct a learned or acquired fault), but it requires ten times as much effort or units of energy to reeducate the dog as was expended in learning the trick (improper act or fault) in the first place. This most valuable contribution to the knowledge of animal behavior must be utilized fully by the trainer who desires to correct a fault in a gun dog.

The most common faults of Springer gun dogs fall into two broad categories. They are (1) those faults or characteristics which are inherited, and (2) those faults or characteristics which are acquired.

Four of the most common inherited faults are: lack of desire to hunt; unwillingness to accept training kindly; poor nose; and, perhaps, the tendency towards hard mouth. Five of the most common acquired faults are gun-shyness; blinking; hunting out of control; breaking shot and flush.

It is possible for a dog to acquire other bad habits which render him unsuitable as a reliable gun dog. But limits of space preclude a discussion of other than the most important ones.

1. Inherited Faults

The worst possible fault that a prospective gun dog can have is the lack of desire to hunt. This condition is to be found in all breeds, and all strains within the breeds, but fortunately it is the exception rather than the rule in Springers (at least in the working strains). The owner of a new puppy should not expect him to start hunting immediately after he is put down in cover. The desire to hunt is an instinct, and it develops slowly in some bloodlines—faster in others. It must be given a chance to manifest itself in the dog, however, by repeated contacts with game. As a rule, no puppy will hunt the first time he is taken into the field, but a dog of almost any breed will learn to hunt if given full opportunity to develop his instincts to do so.

If a young dog between the ages of six months and a year is put on suitable game (birds and rabbits) 15 or 20 times, he will, if normal, eventually put his nose to the ground and start to search for more game to find and chase. If he does not do so, the owner had best consult a professional or good amateur trainer and ask for advice. If an older dog between the ages of one and two years exhibits no interest in hunting after he has been in close proximity to a number of game birds, rabbits, or planted pigeons (say 30 or 40), it would be wise to consult an experienced dog man for advice. If it is determined that the dog has little or no interest in hunting, he should be disposed of promptly to someone looking for a house pet, and be replaced with a dog from a proven hunting strain.

One of the worst things that can happen to any sportsman is to have a gun dog with a poor nose. Fortunately, this does not occur too frequently, but there is little that can be done about it when it does occur. All experienced dog people know that a puppy or Spaniel of any age must first learn to use his nose before a decision can be made as to whether he has a good one or a poor one. According to David Lorenz, of Barrington, Illinois, who has trained gun dogs of all breeds, about half of a dog's scenting ability is in his head. In other words, a dog not only must be born with a good nose, but also must learn to use it.

A young puppy, when he first strikes the scent of game, will often make several stabbing motions in different directions. This is perfectly normal conduct in a green puppy and the trainer should not be discouraged if the dog fails to locate positively the first five or ten times he comes in contact with game. After considerable experience, the dog will be more positive and will go directly to the bird once he takes the scent.

Young dogs are usually not able to follow the trail or scent line of birds, or rabbits either, until some experience has been acquired. They will leave the trail after following it for a few feet or yards, and fail to produce. This is not a fault, for much experience is required for a Spaniel to learn to trail and "catch up" with a running pheasant or rabbit. Most can and do learn it, if given the experience.

It should be remembered that in the late spring and summer, when cover is green, a dog's scenting ability will decrease as much as fifty percent. The same is true even in the autumn, if there has been a long dry spell.

If other dogs appear to scent and find game, but the prospect being trained cannot do so after long and often repeated attempts, the dog should be disposed of and a new prospect acquired. Lack of ability to scent may be inherited or can be the result of a disease such as distemper. Regardless of the reason, it is likely that no improvement will be made, and the dog will be better off as a pet in the home of some friend or neighbor.

One of the most controversial subjects among Spaniel field people is the question of hard mouth. It goes without saying, however, that the Spaniel has a hard mouth if he picks up a dead bird and mangles the carcass to the point that it is not fit for the table. The question which disturbs field trial fans is the dog (and it is not a rare occurrence) which catches a live pheasant or pigeon, and kills the bird while carrying it in to the handler. It is argued by some that this should not be held against the dog because it could never happen in actual hunting. There are others who feel that even though the bird is not damaged enough to ruin it for the table, the dog should still be penalized. Most judges follow a middle ground and assess no penalty unless the bird shows considerable evidence of crushed ribs or a crushed backbone—always the true mark of a real hard-mouthed dog. Mr. Charles Alington wrote a most interesting chapter on hard mouth in his very excellent book, which should be read by all trainers.

There is some evidence to indicate that the *tendency* toward hard mouth is an inherited trait. This is by no means a certainty, but it has been observed that certain Spaniel strains have produced several dogs through as many as five generations which exhibit a tendency toward the fault. For this reason, it would appear that the fault might have some genealogical background. Be that as it may, the best and only positive cure for a genuine case of hard mouth is to prevent it before it develops. This may be done by thoroughly conditioning carrying reflexes until a firmly established habit pattern of quick pickup and fast delivery becomes second nature to the dog. A. P. Moecher, one of the pioneer Springer fanciers in the Middle West, worked out a system for conditioning a dog's retrieving reflexes to the desired degree. His system is described in the chapter in "Preliminary Training of the Gun Dog".

Once a dog acquires the fault of crushing the backbone or rib structure of birds while retrieving, it is most difficult to overcome the habit. Corrective measures may be instituted by preparing a canvas jacket, to which carpet tacks are attached, and requiring the dog to retrieve a dead bird which has been wrapped in the jacket. The results are never positive, although this may work in some cases. Occasionally, a Spaniel that has developed the fault will gradually improve his carry if he has lots of game killed for him. This is not always true, though, and cannot be relied upon 100 percent. Sometimes working the dog in the yard with a clipped-wing pigeon will produce results if the trainer follows the procedure of offering the bird to the dog and taking stern action if the bird is mangled.

Requiring the dog to hold first a dead pigeon, and later a live pigeon, in his mouth in the yard for five or ten minutes at a time will sometimes produce results. If a month or two are devoted to the training, a trainer with patience and understanding may be able to "talk" the dog into holding the bird tenderly and retrieving the same way.

Force breaking to retrieve will also produce results in some cases, but is a procedure best handled by the professional or experienced amateur trainer rather than the novice. The author is not aware of any sure-fire system except that of properly conditioning the dog's reflexes in the beginning.

It is most interesting to note that early writers refer to hard mouth, and it would appear that the fault has been prevalent for many, many years. It is entirely possible that it may have been a desirable trait when Spaniels were used extensively for hawking. Early writers mention that it was the function of the dog to flush the game for the hawk and then be on hand when the hawk dropped to the ground with its prey, in order to hold it until the hunter arrived on the scene. When large birds were the victims of the hawk, it stands to reason that one service a Spaniel could render would be to attack and kill if the hawk had not previously done so.

Fortunately, hard mouth does not appear too often in modern Springers, and most trainers will not be involved in corrective measures.

2. Acquired Faults in Gun Dogs

Perhaps one of the greatest faults that a gun dog can have is the acquired fault of blinking, which is usually man made. Blinking is the disgusting action of a dog that refuses to acknowledge game by flushing or by eagerly questing it. An exhibition of blinking may consist of anything from a slight bit of bird-shyness to an outright refusal to go near a bird. Some blinkers will circle a bird repeatedly, while old, confirmed cases will even avoid a bird they scent, and actually hunt in the opposite direction.

In a human, an act similar to blinking might be called a perversion. It comes under this same classification in gun dogs. It is the worst fault that a gun dog can have outside of downright refusal to hunt.

If a young gun dog exhibits *any* tendency toward bird-shyness (such as a reluctance to flush, or circling a bird repeatedly) the danger signals are flying, and it is time to institute corrective measures. This usually consists of putting the dog in the kennel for a month or two and eliminating all training. At the end of the rest period, training may be resumed with clipped-wing pigeons. The dog should be encouraged to catch the pigeons and to chase rabbits to his heart's desire. When he retrieves the birds or chases a rabbit, he should be made over and petted profusely. If he refuses to give chase, the trainer can set an example by running after the game and exhibiting great animation and excitement.

The clipped-wing birds can be thrown for retrieving in the yard and when the bird flutters and attempts to escape, most young blinkers will overcome their perversion enough to give chase and to show some interest. Such action must be encouraged and every aid given to the dog to restore his confidence. Sometimes blinking occurs in a very young puppy which is introduced to game too early. The sound of the pheasant or pigeon beating its wings as it flushes may frighten a shy young dog. One solution here is to keep the dog away from game until he is older. Good results are usually obtained with clipped-wing birds in the yard if the prospect is six or more months old. Younger dogs should be allowed to mature before they are exposed to game again if they show fright the first time or two they are in contact with a flushing bird. Exposing the young blinker to birds gradually and giving him much praise will serve to build up his confidence. Also, working him with another dog may prove beneficial. Blinking that results from training methods which are too severe or too advanced may be cured if corrective measures are started before the fault becomes fixed as a habit.

The terrible fault of gun-shyness is usually considered a man-made one, although some animal research people came up with the theory a few years ago that it might be inherited. Very few experienced trainers will agree with this theory, however. A dog becomes gun-shy when confused and thus fails to comprehend why the gun is fired. If one follows the suggestion outlined in Section I of the chapter on preliminary training, the chances are 100 to 1 that gun-shyness will never be a problem.

When the condition is observed, the first thing to do is to stop all work and to return the dog to the kennel for a few days' rest. The trainer should think back and try to recall the events that may have caused the confusion in the dog's mind. Naturally, repetition of the events that frightened and confused the dog should be avoided at all cost. If the subject is only six or eight months old, the hand clapping procedure outlined in the chapter on preliminary training should be started, and mixed with kind treatment. If the trainer is persistent, this will probably help overcome the dog's fear of the noise. This statement is based not only on practical experience, but also on sound psychological fact. The simultaneous application of two stimuli will serve to condition the dog to accept the lesser, which in this case will be the hand clap. If the dog really loves to retrieve, the trainer can then progress by easy stages to the use of the cap pistol (at feeding time or when the dog is retrieving).

If enough time is taken, and the lessons are carefully and widely spaced, the dog will respond as desired and in a month or two may be introduced gradually to the 20 gauge shotgun again. If the prospect is older and exhibits fear or nervousness when the shotgun stage has been reached, he should be taken back to the yard, started over with the hand clapping, and worked up progressively through the cap pistol, the .22 blanks, and the shotgun.

If the gun-shy dog is older and represents an extreme case of gun-shyness, the condition may be corrected by the old and often used method of discharging a cap pistol or .22 blank at feeding time. The theory behind this method is the well-established psychological principle of associating two stimuli (one good and one bad) simultaneously. The bad becomes associated with the good in the dog's mind and the fault is thus corrected or overcome.

To introduce this procedure, food is offered to the dog and a cap pistol is fired immediately when he starts to eat. If he leaves the feed pan and cowers in his kennel, the trainer should speak a few encouraging words and urge the dog to eat. When he again starts to eat, the pistol should again be fired. This is usually enough to drive the dog away from the food for good, and the trainer should then remove the pan and offer the animal no more food until the next day. At this time the above procedure should be repeated and the same action followed. If the dog refuses to eat after the cap pistol has been fired a time or two, the trainer must harden his heart and again remove the food.

Usually, after three or four days the dog's hunger will overcome his fear of the gun and he will gulp his food rapidly even if the cap pistol is fired several times. The lesson should be repeated each time the dog is fed until he has learned to eat without flinching. This may require several weeks or months, but the system is sure and will work if the trainer is persistent.

As a salve to the trainer's conscience, it may be said that while this method is severe, it will rehabilitate the dog to a normal life. Gun-shy dogs go through life flinching from automobile backfires or other common noises, and their existence is one of abject fear and anguish. Realizing that he is helping to rehabilitate the dog to live a normal fear-free life may help the trainer harden his heart in the early stages. It is a cinch that the dog will eventually become hungry enough to eat no matter how often the gun is fired. And that is the secret of the cure.

The ability to mark accurately the "fall" of a bird and to retrieve it with dispatch is a most valuable attribute of any gun dog. Springer Spaniels that refuse to retrieve are only performing half of the job. Their refusal to perform this function is usually due to the fact that they have not been trained to retrieve or because they associate some unpleasant experience with the act. The first cause is relatively simple to overcome, but the latter is more difficult.

If a young puppy refuses to retrieve, the trainer should first make sure that some member of the household is not throwing sticks or other objects and failing to follow through by accepting the object when the dog returns with it. After this possibility has been eliminated, the puppy should be started on the routine suggested in the chapter on preliminary training. If the dog shows no interest in running after a thrown object, such as an old glove or the buck, it will be necessary for the trainer to spend considerable time in an attempt to arouse interest. A towel can be dragged along the ground and the puppy allowed to pounce on it. When he becomes interested, the towel should be knotted once or twice, then tossed for the dog while he is in full pursuit. The trainer should never engage in a tug of war with the puppy but should tease him just enough to arouse his interest and then throw the object slowly. The procedure outlined in the chapter on preliminary training can then be followed.

If the Springer has not been started on retrieving until he is two or three years of age, he may exhibit little or no interest at first. His interest may be aroused by having another dog retrieve in very close proximity to the backward pupil.

A number of years ago, a friend brought a Springer bitch about seven years old to the author's home. Patty was a good hunter but would not retrieve. She would run to the bird and stand over it until her owner came to pick it up. On the day in question, repeated attempts were made to get Patty to retrieve a dead pigeon. She refused point-blank. Several other Springers were then brought out and permitted to retrieve in the presence of Patty. After fifteen minutes of this work, the bird was thrown and Patty retrieved it promptly. Six weeks later she was a good retriever.

It is a well-established fact that dogs can learn certain acts by observation. It is also a well-established fact that dogs are subject to jealousy. They can learn to hunt, to retrieve, and to react in certain desired (also undesired) ways by imitating the actions of another dog. Experienced trainers take full advantage of this fact in working with their dogs.

If a Springer suddenly stops retrieving after he has been performing the act for some time, the trouble may usually be diagnosed as resulting from some bad experience which the dog has associated with the act. In such cases, it is probably well to permit the dog to rest for a period of several weeks. He can then be started on the basic or pre-retrieving routine outlined in the chapter on preliminary training. Plenty of patience and copious use of kind words and petting will usually bring him around in time. The trainer should be cautioned against giving up too early. Any dog can be taught to retrieve if the trainer is persistent and kind. However, the dog with his tail between his legs and a hangdog expression is an indication that the trainer has used too much force—unconscious force, perhaps, but still too much. The trainer must relax and make the training a game. Since every dog can be taught to retrieve, it is the trainer's fault in most cases if the dog fails to respond.

Hunting out of control, which means working well out of gunshot range, is usually the result or lack of early training. When a Springer prospect works in such a manner, two simple corrective measures are required: (1) he should be worked only into the wind for a month or two; and (2) he should be taught to turn on the whistle. The training technique to teach both are outlined in detail in the chapter on intermediate field work. If a dog will turn on the whistle *every* time and has learned the simple hand signals, it is an easy matter to get him to hunt within range in the desired pattern. The use of the whistle and the work into the wind alone will usually produce the required pattern of work. The trainer must be sure, however, that the dog knows and understands the whistle signal perfectly, and then must insist that he respond.

Breaking to shot and/or wing is a serious fault and a clear indication that the dog's early training in the yard has not been learned thoroughly. Even though the culprit may be of mature age, the best solution to the problem is to return to the early yard training and to progress along the lines previously suggested in the several chapters on training. If they have little or no work between the annual shooting seasons, many hunting Springers develop the habit of breaking to shot or wing after having been steady. This may be due to the fact that the owner relaxed his efforts and permitted the dog to retrieve a few times without the command. If such is the case, a refresher course is in order, with a new start being made on the early yard work. Usually the desired results can be obtained by a day or two devoted to each step, if the trainer is firm and does not permit the dog to complete any retrieve in the yard or field until ordered to do so.

There are several electronic devices on the market consisting of a special dog collar by which the trainer can deliver by remote control a light electrical shock to a dog that is some distance away. Undoubtedly such devices have merit in special cases, but their use is NOT recommended for the novice trainer. They should be used sparingly, and only by a professional or experienced amateur who understands principles of animal psychology and the temperament of the individual dog.

There are other faults that a dog may acquire. Most of them can be corrected by going back to the fundamentals and treating the dog just as if he were to be started on his early training again. Not as much time need be spent on each step as with a brand new prospect, but each lesson should be repeated until the dog is exhibiting the desired qualities of obedience, control, and enthusiasm. The absence of any one is fatal to a top gun dog.

Bill Brauer and noted outdoor writer David Michael Duffy with bag of 12 Canadian sharptail grouse flushed and retrieved by Duffy's favorite Springer, Flirt. Duffy's book, *Hunting Dog Know-How,* has no equal.

Joe Crooks and Virginia Diegel wth 12 Oregon ducks proudly retrieved by the still wet Sunny of Silvercreek. Springers are fine water dogs.

9

How To Hunt Game and Waterfowl with a Springer Spaniel

THE Springer Spaniel gun dog is equally at home on land or water, and on fur or feathers. He is, however, the pheasant dog *par excellence,* and has no peers (nor has he had for the past several hundred years) in this hunting. His greatest usefulness on upland game is as a beater who will sweep back and forth on a 50 to 80 yard front, five to ten yards in front of the gun or guns. A well-trained Springer will drop (sit) to flush and/or, shot and retrieve only on command. He is equally at home on native game or when used on released game at a shooting preserve.

The Springer Spaniel is, in our opinion based on considerable experience with the several hunting breeds, the top pheasant dog in the United States. When hunted on native pheasant during the best shooting hours (the hour after sunrise or the three hours before sunset) when birds are feeding, he should always be worked into the wind when possible. This will keep him closer to the hunter and require less handling by whistle or voice. Stubble fields or picked corn fields are natural feeding places for pheasant, but difficult for the quartering dog to handle since birds can see the hunter for 100 yards or more and are likely to run rather than hide. Under such conditions one or two hunting companions should be stationed at the far end of the field to "block". Running birds or those which the dog and gun flush wild can be taken by the blockers. There will always be a bird or two which skulks along the fence or ditch at the end of the field and a good Springer will use his nose and push them out fast as well as those which attempt to hide or duck back.

In light cover, running birds will require some handling to keep the eager Springer within gun range. He will have a nose full of feathers and want to go. Spaniels should quarter under such conditions, but if the temptation is great, because of good scenting, let him get out to medium gun range (30 yards), then sit him down with one blast of the whistle and hurry to him. Then cast him out to resume his trailing of the hot scent. Sometimes it will require several stops and fast walking before the Spaniel can flush in gun range.

After the first day of the pheasant season the birds become wary and often take to heavy wet sloughs where movement is difficult for Spaniel and man. In such conditions give the dog his head and don't insist on quartering. The rough ground will usually enable the hunter to keep up as the dog zigzags after the hopping birds, who may circle, duck back, or use numerous tricks to avoid flying. An experienced dog will eventually put the bird up for a shot.

Soil bank or uncut hay fields are ideal spots to work a Springer. Pheasant roost in such places and rest in them during the middle of the day. However, an hour or two after sunrise and before sunset are the most productive hours to hunt.

When working pheasants in standing corn, it is usually the wise procedure to make the dog heel as the several members of the shooting party spread out and drive down the field. When within 50 yards of the end, cast the Spaniel to the right or left and keep him quartering. Often he will raise a bird or two in the fence row at the end, but if game is exceptionally wary and wild, a blocker stationed at the end will usually get a shot.

Hunting doves with a Spaniel conserves game, because the dog will find most, if not all, of the birds that are dropped, whereas 50% is par for the dogless dove shooter. An ideal spot is the edge of a feed patch, (stubble field, picked corn, etc.) adjacent to a water hole. Pre-season cruising will enable the smart hunter to locate several such spots that doves are using. When the flight pattern is determined, the gunner should conceal himself in a fence row or against a tree, with the Springer sitting at heel. When the morning or evening flight begins it will be fast and furious, and it's well to keep the dog at heel until there are several birds on the ground before sending him to retrieve. He will learn to remember the last one or two downed but may need direction on others. Doves will seldom flair from a moving dog, so don't worry if Rover is too excited to wait until several are downed. When doves want to come in to feed, or to a water hole, nothing can really keep them out—early in the season. The experienced Springer will learn to search the skies, and when he sees incoming flights or pairs his furious tail action and eyes will reveal the fact.

Spaniels have a special love for rabbits which are found in fence rows, briar patches adjacent to cover and feed, brush piles, hay, grain, or stubble fields. When hunting open fields, keep the dog quartering and work into the wind. Let the dog work the brush piles but stay on the opposite side. When hunting fence rows, let the dog work the fence line for 10–20 yards, then swing him out with hand or whistle to the right or left. He may pick up a rabbit away from the fence. Such tactics will help keep him in gun range. It's wise to keep the dog moving, rather than let him potter with a low head on last night's stale scent. An experienced Spaniel will let the hunter know soon enough when he strikes hot ground scent. When working a Springer on any type of game, keep him MOVING. When he strikes hot scent of either fur or feathers, his head will go down and he'll be off like a shot. When close enough to take the body scent, his head will come up as he dives in to flush. If permitted to potter on old scent much trouble can result.

Shooting game birds in timber with a Spaniel is great sport. We will describe the Springers work on woodcock and ruffed grouse as if they were the same bird, even though their habits are slightly different. In early autumn shooting of either bird, they are likely to be found in medium to heavy timber and underbrush. Since it is difficult to keep track of an eager Spaniel in timber, some hunters "bell" their dogs. Spaniels achieved great renown as woodcock dogs in Britain in the Middle Ages and with experience can still fill the game bag.

The dog should beat the cover in timber as he does in more open terrain, except his casts to the side should be reduced to 15–20 yards by handling. In exceptionally heavy early fall cover he will squirm under and through most productively and move out birds which might never be flushed otherwise. Later in the autumn as the leaves and ground foliage die, the experienced Springer will automatically increase the distance of his side casts and cover more ground. When game is shot and the dog sent to retrieve, often a dog will refuse his first woodcock. But a five minute retrieving lesson in which the shot bird is thrown a half dozen times, and the dog encouraged to retrieve, will overcome this difficulty in short order.

Years ago, in the Wisconsin woods, one of our Spaniels flushed a woodcock which towered, fell, and lodged in a spruce tree unknown to us. We ordered the dog to the vicinity repeatedly, and when our

Gibraltar Dignity, flushed and retrieved hundreds of pheasant, quail and waterfowl for owner Val Durvin, as well as winning 46 trophies in Western field trials.

shooting partner located the dead cock in the tree we learned a valuable lesson about trusting the dog. Keep the Spaniel moving from side to side in timber and listen for the bell when he is out of sight. The tempo of its sound will often tell you exactly what the dog is doing. Use hand signals to direct him in all hunting when possible. The human voice disturbs game. Use the whistle when he can't see you, but use it sparingly. Too much whistle disturbs game, and may make the dog immune to its command.

There are four types of waterfowl shooting in which a Spaniel may be used most effectively:

1. Shooting from a blind over decoys
2. Pass shooting
3. Jump shooting
4. Shooting from a boat.

Shooting from a blind is the most common method in each of the four great fly-ways. We expect our Spaniels to sit quietly without whining or moving and with his head in the special "dog-door" at one end of the blind. A young dog may need to be leashed his first year to prevent bolting when game is downed, but if thoroughly trained and firmly handled the leash can be eliminated after a few trips to the blind. When a flight comes in, never send the dog to retrieve until things slow down a bit, since ducks usually won't work the blocks with a dog splashing around near them. Obviously with several ducks down for a half hour or longer the Spaniel will have to be directed to some of them, but he'll improve his area of search with experience and will find the cripple which came to life and tried to dive or sneak down the shore.

Pass shooting with a Spaniel is much like dove shooting, except the dog should *always* be well hidden from sight. Between flights, he can be allowed to retrieve the dead and cripples, which he will trail out with dispatch. Occasionally "Rover" will need a little "refresher" course in manners if the action is fast, but do it thoroughly, and don't nag him all day because it will ruin the shoot for you and your shooting companions. A well-conditioned Spaniel can work in temperatures down to 10–20 above zero. We usually have an old piece of "tarp" to cover our dogs on cold, blustery days.

Jump shooting with a Spaniel on any species of waterfowl is great fun. When working large marsh areas it is well to keep the Spaniel at heel because even a well-conditioned one may run out of gas as he half swims, walks, and jumps through much heavy, aquatic vegetation. When a duck or snipe or lone goose is jumped, "Rover" will soon learn to stand on his back legs at the crack of the gun to mark the fall. At the command to "Fetch!" he will slither off through the marsh grass in the direction of the fall. If he fails to mark for any reason, direct him to the fall with hand signals as described in the chapters on training.

Working a Spaniel from a boat can be tricky. Small duck boats are out, of course, but he can be used satisfactorily in a beamy craft which won't capsize when he leaves or enters after a retrieve. The dog should never be chained to the boat because he can drown both of you if he should fall or jump in while on the leash. Instead, he must be taught to sit quietly in one spot and to remain there at all times. There can be no exceptions to this rule. Frankly, we only use Spaniels from a boat on rare occasions, and it is not really a recommended procedure.

There have been shooting preserves in America for many, many years but the quantities have increased tremendously since World War II. Most of these establishments, regardless of whether private, semi-private, or public, release pen-raised pheasant, quail, or chucker partridge at frequent intervals for the members. Almost all have strict rules about the dogs which are used, because an untrained dog of any breed can ruin the shooting for everyone in the area. Working a Spaniel

Mrs. Evelyn Monte, well known writer and sportswoman, chats with Aidan Roark as FTC Rex On The Rocks listens intently. Roark was a top U.S. polo player before he became interested in Springer gun dogs.

Belaston Camac Ruff and Belaston Buccaneer. These two fine Amateur Field Champions are owned by Jim Richie of Ohio.

on a walk-up type shoot is much like hunting him on wild birds. He should quarter the ground in front of the guns like a windshield wiper, and not bore out down the field. Working into the wind will help prevent "punching out", since all dogs—both domestic and wild—naturally swing out further down wind than upwind when hunting. It is most important to keep the Spaniel under control to preserve shooting since there is usually much more game and more people present. Loud shouting and whistling are most undesirable. Keep the dog under control, and don't take him along unless he is under excellent control. It's bad etiquette, and may be embarrassing if you are asked to take him out of the field.

Many preserves have pass duck shooting in which duck are released. This may be a combination of pass and blind shooting with the former more prevalent. Again keep the Spaniel at heel and under control. Send him to retrieve during lulls in the shooting and never—repeat, *never*—let him run wild and steal shot birds from a nearby station or blind.

Cover at some preserves is grown and/or cut in narrow strips. Since experienced Spaniels seldom like to leave the strips of cover, the wise, courteous handler will keep his Spaniel at heel, and if it is necessary to fight him to cross to the adjacent strip on each cast, use him strictly for retrieving. Working a normal 30–50 yard front in row-stripped areas requires training and experience. Condition your dog to such conditions when you are alone and won't disturb the countryside, and all the game and people therein.

The great British sire, Eng. FTC Rivington Glensaugh Glean. He sired 12 English and American Field Champions plus many winners and top shooting dogs. He won six British Open Stakes and the British National Field Championship. A great field dog and sire.

10
Why Field Trials for Springer Spaniel Gun Dogs?

F IELD TRIALS for Spaniels are competitive hunting contests, in which released game is substituted for native game in order to provide each dog with equal opportunity. The dogs are worked in braces on parallel courses, but do not cooperate with each other. The handler of each dog is accompanied by an official gunner and a judge. All dogs that perform creditably in the first series are called back for further testing in a second series (under the other judge), and in Championship All Age Stakes, may be called back for a third series with both judges observing one dog simultaneously.

The Spaniels (and not their handlers) are under judgment, and are scored on: their ability and desire to hunt and to find game; the width of their hunting pattern, and the way they cover the ground; the degree in which they work to the gun and their response to hand, voice, or whistle command; their ability to flush and mark the fall of shot game; their steadiness to flush and shot; and their ability to find and retrieve with a soft mouth all game shot for them.

The events normally scheduled by any of the thirty Spaniel clubs in the United States are a Puppy Stake, followed perhaps by a Shooting Dog Stake (handler does own shooting), an Amateur All Age Stake and an Open All Age Stake. Both of the All Age Stakes carry cham-

The veteran sportsman Tom Fussell with FTC
Tangles Pandora. Fussell trained and handled this
excellent Springer bitch to both Open and Amateur Field Championships.

Mrs. Ruth Greening and Mrs. Jean Hutchenson, two excellent
women handlers. The Springers are AFTCs that the ladies trained
and handled to their titles.

pionship points, and the winner of two in each category acquires the title of either Amateur Field Champion or Open Field Champion. Trophies and ribbons are awarded winning and placing dogs, plus qualifying certificates for each of the National Championship events. The titles A.F.C. or F.C. in any pedigree are highly meaningful and the *only* titles the prospective owner of a Spaniel gun dog should look for or accept.

To answer the novice who asks, "Why Field Trials?", we can detail 100 reasons, but the broad appeal is the sport of breeding and/or training a high class gun dog with which the owner can compete against other sportsmen with similar ideas. We have hundreds of friends in trials in all sections of the country who will say they want a better hunting dog, that they enjoy the outdoor recreation, that it improves their shooting and hunting lore, or that it's thrilling and exciting to train and handle a hunting dog. All are good sound, acceptable reasons. However, the sport of shooting game over dogs is a basic motivation. Moreover, the field trial fancier stretches the shooting season for a few weeks to many months, since he can usually find an excuse for working his dog on planted game several times each week or month, depending on the degree of his addiction. Many of our friends belong to Spaniel Clubs at which one can find a kindred soul in the training areas 52 Saturdays and Sundays each year. Obviously, such individuals become top wing shots (a dozen dogs will be worked on 50–75 birds each session and the birds have to be shot). There are, of course, "golf widows", "fishing widows", and "spectator sport widows", but there are few "Spaniel widows" because Mama often joins the head of the family when he takes "Rover" to the field for training. Some of the gals get so attached to the family gun dog Spaniel that they get in the act, too. Many have done exceptionally well, and Mrs. Joe Crooks in California is an outstanding example. She and Joe have two Field Champions and Doris put the first win on each of them, with Joe handling both dogs to their second (easier?) win.

Mrs. Evelyn Bui, dedicated editor of *The Springer Bark.* This remarkable publication reports on all facets of Springer Spaniel activity in a most professional manner.

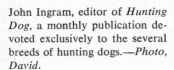

John Ingram, editor of *Hunting Dog,* a monthly publication devoted exclusively to the several breeds of hunting dogs.—*Photo, David.*

William F. Brown, editor of *The American Field* magazine. Brown is an authority on the several breeds of gun dogs and the author of numerous books and articles on gun dogs.

Selected Reading

*Publications of value for the
trainer and shooting man*

United States Periodicals of Value to Sportsmen:

THE AMERICAN FIELD, a weekly which reports field trial results
of several breeds as well as factual information of interest to
the sportsman. (William Brown, *Editor,* 222 W. Adams St., Chicago, Ill. 60606.)

THE SPRINGER BARK, a quarterly devoted exclusively to English
Springer Spaniels in the field, on the bench, and in the Obedience
ring. (Mrs. Evelyn Bui, *Editor,* Box 817, San Leandro, Calif.
94577.)

HUNTING DOG, a monthly with broad coverage of practically all
the hunting breeds. The emphasis, as name implies, is on hunting.
(John Ingram, *Editor,* Box 330, Greenfield, Ohio 45123.)

Books on Gun Dog Training
(Published in the United States):

THE INTERNATIONAL ENCYCLOPEDIA OF DOGS. *Edited by
Stanley Dangerfield and Elsworth S. Howell.* A modern up-to-date
compilation about facts about many breeds in many countries, told
in a comprehensible manner.

THE MODERN DOG ENCYCLOPEDIA *by Henry Davis.* An outstanding, comprehensive work covering history, breeding and training of all breeds in all phases of their activity.

HUNTING DOG KNOW-HOW *by David Michael Duffy.* A first
class work on the several gun dog breeds by a practical hunter
who knows what to say and how to say it.

THE SPRINGER SPANIEL *by Maxwell Riddle*. A well-organized book covering bench, field, and obedience tests for Spaniels. Bloodline charts of leading Springer sires.

TRAINING YOUR SPANIEL *by Clarence Pfaffenberger*. A good manual for the novice Spaniel owner.

ANIMAL BEHAVIOR *by John Paul Scott*. A psychological explanation of animal behavior.

GENETICS AND THE SOCIAL BEHAVIOR OF THE DOG *by John Paul Scott* and *John L. Fuller*.

SHOOTING PRESERVE MANAGEMENT—THE NYLO SYSTEM *by Edward L. Kozicky* and *John Madson*. A comprehensive discussion of preserve management containing much information of value to the preserve shooter.

THE TRUTH ABOUT SPORTING DOGS *by C. Bede Maxwell*. A well-written book, oriented to the dual potential of the Sporting breeds.

British Books of Value to the Spaniel Trainer:

SPANIELS FOR SPORT *by Talbot Radcliffe*. One of the best training manuals in existence, in which Radcliffe—a highly successful British Springer breeder—up-dates the classic work of H. W. Carlton, *Spaniels:* Their Breaking for Sport and Field Trials.

FIELD TRIALS AND JUDGING *by Charles Alington*. Will broaden the knowledge of any shooting man who works with dogs.

TRAINING AND FIELD TRIALS *by P. R. A. Moxon*. A fine training manual by a professional gun dog trainer.

DOG TRAINING BY AMATEURS *by R. Sharpe*. One of the classic works on how to train a Spaniel gun dog.

The late Freeman Lloyd, pioneer Springer advocate and writer in America.

Maxwell Riddle, famous author and widely respected all-breed judge.

SECTION II

Show and Obedience Springers

by

Julia Gasow

Julia Gasow

To my husband,
Fred

to whose unselfish love, continual encour-
agement and ever-dependable help I owe
whatever success I've enjoyed in the sport
of dogs—and who, more than anyone else,
has helped keep it fun for me.

Introduction to the
Show Springer Section

WE ARE PLEASED, and flattered, to have been asked to provide a presentation of the show English Springer Spaniel for this revised edition of Mr. Charles Goodall's classic work on the breed. That the field and the conformation Springer are really of two different "worlds" is today indisputable, and the recognition of this in providing this new section for *The New English Springer Spaniel* does indeed make the book more complete and—we hope—more serviceable.

The wide scope of the book necessarily limits the depth with which we can treat the history of the show Springer. Other recent works, most notably the fine edition of *"The English Springer Spaniel in North America"*, published by the parent club of the breed—the English Springer Spaniel Field Trial Association, Inc., comprehensively cover the year-by-year statistics for those who seek greater historical detail. We have here limited ourselves to the high spots, to just the consideration of the dogs that have been a principal influence on today's competitors.

While we have paid some attention to the winning of these dogs, we have aimed to put a greater stress on their production. It was interesting, for example, that in studying the background of the top ten winners in 1969, we noted that all of them—without exception—stemmed from the ten dogs that we had selected as being the most significant in the period from 1945 until then.

Obviously, in being this selective, personal opinion becomes a factor. We have tried to be fair, and all-inclusive, but at the same time we have occasionally offered some frank evaluations based upon close to forty years of experience with the breed. For those who see it differently, we can only say that these are the judgments that have worked best for us at Salilyn.

For the sake of interest, we have tried to keep the presentation as pictorial as possible. Almost every dog mentioned is pictured, and in many cases pedigrees are also included for those who would use this book as a breeding beacon.

We hope that the pictorial section on grooming, and the question-and-answer chapter on dog care are helpful. In the latter, we have tried to include the questions that have been most frequently asked by those who have purchased dogs from our kennels over the years.

Helping compose a book has been something new for us, and we are grateful to many who helped make the challenge a bit easier. We particularly want to thank Fred Hunt and George Pugh for their help with the copy. Our dear friend, Mary Valentine, typed the manuscript as a labor of love. And our thanks, too, to the many fellow Springer enthusiasts who have cooperated so wholeheartedly in sending us pictures and pedigrees of their notable dogs.

—Julia Gasow

Julia (Mrs. Fred H.) Gasow has been a breeder of show English Springer Spaniels since the early 1930s, and is today one of the most respected judges of the breed. Her Salilyn Kennels has accounted for more than 100 champions and more than a dozen all-breed Best in Show awards. She has been honored with the Kennel Review award as "Dog Breeder of the Year", and in 1971 was voted "Dog Woman of the Year", considered by many to be the highest accolade in the sport.

An historic photo—the first English Springer Spaniel Specialty at Englewood, New Jersey in 1922. W. J. Hutchinson, a pioneer in American interest in the breed, is third from the right, and the famous writer and breed advocate, Freeman Lloyd, is at far right.—*Photo by Rudolph W. Tauskey, and presented by Mr. Tauskey to Mrs. Gasow.*

11

Bench Springers in America

THE FIRST SPECIALTY SHOW for English Springer Spaniels in the United States was held at Englewood, New Jersey in 1922. The exhibits were field trial dogs—their owners great sportsmen, to be remembered for their contribution to both bench and field.

These gentlemen ran their dogs in a field trial one day, combed out the burrs, and then the following day showed them for conformation. However, this first Specialty touched off a spark of enthusiasm for the joy of winning on Springer beauty as well as field ability.

Fanciers continued to run and show their dogs successfully as late as the early 1930s. But more and more they became critical of the overall appearance of the "non-conformist" field trial Springer, whose owner was interested in only that one phase of the sport. They became aware of the importance of coat and feather in the ring, and a show-minded individual no longer cared to subject his prospective winner to the general hazards of field work.

This was the beginning of a division in Springer type, represented by two distinct sports within the breed. Over the years, these groups have grown farther apart, with some resulting friction along the way.

Many felt that this division would be the ruination of the breed, but results have proved quite the contrary. Each of the two phases has become so highly specialized that we now have English Springer Spaniel superiority on two fronts, as it were: ability unsurpassed by any other

English, American and Canadian
Champion Springbok of Ware

Dual Ch. Flint of Avandale, whelped 1921. Springbok and Flint were the
most prominent of the many Springers imported to America by Eudore
Chevrier of Canada.

breed in field trials, and a bench record unmatched by any other breed since 1967.

Today field trial enthusiasts and bench enthusiasts are pretty much agreed that each dog does best within its own sphere, and that neither does well the work of the other. It is also agreed that the field trial dog is too high strung to make a good house dog.

From personal experience I can advise against crossing these two strains if your aim is to produce a show-winning Springer that can compete creditably in field trials. From the first breeding of such a cross it would take at least four generations back to bench breeding to have a show dog. By this time, naturally, the speed and field ability gained would be lost. It is easy to produce an excellent hunting dog from bench breeding, but almost impossible to breed a show Springer from field trial stock.

Salilyn's Tarus (at 3 1/2 months), a cross of bench and field breeding.

Significant Bench Springers of the 1920s and Early 1930s

Most active in the importation of many English Springer Spaniels that began in the early 1920s was Eudore Chevrier of Canada. Mr. Chevrier bought extensively, and did well with the breed in Canada under the banner of "Avandale" (often confused with the English kennel name "Avendale".) Most notable of the many he imported were Dual Ch. Flint of Avendale, bred by the Duke of Hamilton, and Eng. Am. & Can. Ch. Springbok of Ware. But in sum, Mr. Chevrier's dogs

Eng. and Am. Ch. Nuthill Dignity,
1930 Best in Show winner.

Am. & Can. Ch. Norman of Hamsey, the first English
Springer to win the Sporting Group at Westminster (in
1933). Owned by the Blue Leader Kennels of Santa
Barbara, California.

Ch. Woodelf of Breeze, Dignity's daughter, behind many of our top-winning Springers of today.

were a heterogeneous lot. He was basically an importer—not a breeder—and established no set line.

In 1928, E. de K. Leffingwell, a Californian, imported Ch. Nuthill Dignity from England. Dignity became a tri-international champion. He had an outstandingly beautiful head—good enough to outweigh the fact that he was, reportedly, somewhat spindly, with weak pasterns and a curly coat. He was a fine showman, and did top winning on both coasts through the early 1930s, including Best of Breed at Westminster in 1930.

Dignity was an important sire as well. Mrs. Betty Buchanan, Breeze Kennels, Denver, Colorado, bred her Dilkusha Darkie to him to produce the ever-remembered bitch, Ch. Woodelf of Breeze, behind so many winning Springers of today.

Robert Elliot also used Nuthill Dignity to advantage at his Elysian Kennels. Dignity is the grandsire of the famous Elysian quintuplets, one of which—King Lion—became the first dual champion in America.

Tragically, Nuthill Dignity got loose one day and ran to the mountains and was never seen again.

Eng., Am. & Can. Ch. Showman of Shotton,
imported from England in 1939 by Paul Quay.

Ch. Runor's Agent, pic-
tured with his owner
Norman Morrow, after
win of the Group at
Trenton.

One of the important English imports, although a somewhat controversial one, was English, American and Canadian Champion Showman of Shotton, brought over in 1939 by Paul Quay of Chagrin Falls, Ohio.

Showman's winning career started immediately upon his arrival. He was shown exclusively by one of the leading handlers in the country, Billy Lang, who later became a licensed all-breed judge, and then an American Kennel Club field representative. Billy campaigned Showman extensively, piloting him to many Best in Show wins in an era before the Springer's great popularity as a Group dog.

Though outstanding in the show ring, Showman's influence on the breed remains questionable. The West Coast profited from him by establishing his powerful rear movement in their bloodlines. In the East, Norman Morrow's best winner, Ch. Runor's Agent, a great moving dog, was sired by him. But Norman himself said of his dog, "Agent was short in foreface and neck and had a somewhat harsh expression."

Billy Lang wrote, well after Showman's retirement, "Showman of Shotton was a mean-eyed rascal and contributed nothing in the way of soft expressive eyes to the breed." Edward Dana Knight, well-known breeder-judge, wrote: "Let's face it—Showman is the greatest disaster that's ever happened to American Springers. There were many things to like about him, but he sired a high percentage of shy dogs and an astonishing number with bad feet."

Ch. Clarion Rufton Tandy (at 9 months of age). This bitch is said to have been the model for the 1932 standard revision.

Ch. Elysian Emissary, 1934 Best in Show winner.

Ch. Timpanogos Melinda, winner of the Sporting Group at West-minster, 1942. Owned by R. E. Allen, and handled by Harry Sangster.

Mr. Charles Toy, whose Clarion Kennels was named for the country in which he lived—about sixty miles from Pittsburgh, was doing much to improve the breed with his English imports during this whole period. Such Springers as Clarion Rufton Trumpet and Clarion Rufton Tandy were great then, and I think would look good today. As a matter of fact, the latter was used as a "model" for the revision of the English Springer standard in 1932.

Mr. Toy's close friend, R. E. Allen of Provo, Utah, a highly respected breeder of champions, did well for the Springer cause with his Timpanogos dogs. Possibly his best were Ch. Melinda, Group winner at Westminster in 1942, and Ch. Timpanogos Radar.

And I must certainly mention George Higgs, whose Boghurst Springers were winning then and are still in the rings today.

There were many other winners at the time, but they have left little, if any, imprint on the breed. The dogs, generally, were longer in body than our present Springer. They were short on leg with poor fronts. Most were heavily ticked.

A representative winner of the time—Ch. Adonis of Avandale.

The immortal Eng. and Am. Ch. Rufton Recorder.

12

The Recorder Influence

ENG. & AM. CH. RUFTON RECORDER
(Boss of Glasnevin ex Rufton Flirt)
Whelped May 11, 1926

ENGLISH and AMERICAN CHAMPION RUFTON RECORDER had the greatest impact of any single dog on our show Springer of today. He was purchased by Fred M. Hunt directly from his English breeder, R. Cornthwaite, and imported to this country in 1933.

Mr. Hunt was well known to the dog world long before this date. He had established his Green Valley Kennels in the beautiful farm lands of Devon, Pennsylvania, had produced several show champions, and for years had taken an active and enthusiastic part in field trials.

Mr. Hunt had purchased Recorder strictly for breeding purposes. The dog was seven years old at the time and therefore an unlikely show prospect. But Recorder was an English show champion, and his sire— Boss of Glasnevin—had been a field trial winner, at one time considered the top prospect in England. Thus Recorder had everything to offer Fred's breeding program.

Very shortly after this great dog's arrival in America it became evident that he was not too old for the show ring, after all. He was active, gay, in good physical condition—in fact, Fred felt that he was the best Springer he had ever seen.

Accordingly, he entered him in several shows and Recorder immediately created a sensation. Many exhibitors were highly critical of him—not surprising, really, for he was very different from the dogs they were producing. He represented change—a "new model" Springer that

Dual Ch. Green Valley Punch. Below, Punch is pictured retrieving a pheasant for his owner, Fred Hunt.

some refused to accept. But the more serious breeders recognized in him quality and style not to be surpassed during the era.

He was taller than his competitors and far more compact, standing on well-boned, perfectly straight forelegs that offered great breed improvement. And his feet were excellent. Though plain in head, his appearance was enhanced by a collar and markings of pure, sparkling white, making him stand out against the heavily ticked dogs of the day.

I am grateful to have seen him shown in 1934 at the English Springer Spaniel Club of Michigan's first Specialty Show, where he was Best of Breed from the limit class (now extinct) over 104 entries. The judge was Freeman Lloyd. Recorder finished his championship in record time.

Since names of Rufton Recorder's direct descendants appear many times in the pedigrees of our current winners, it is interesting to know how they came about, remembering, of course, that we can only touch the high spots in the space allowed us here.

Mr. Hunt leased Woodelf of Breeze, a Nuthill Dignity daughter for two breedings to Recorder. The first produced the most famous litter in Springer history, consisting of six bench show champions. One was Green Valley Punch, who also achieved a Field Trial Championship in 1938. We have not had another dual champion Springer in America since. The other five bench champions were all important winners and all good producers.

One bitch in the litter was never shown. Her bone was fine, and her head unattractive. Her eyes, small and slanting, suggested the name given her—"Orientia". But although not herself show material, Orientia is significant because of her progeny.

Ch. Green Valley Oak, an important producer.

Ch. Dunoon Donald Dhu, Best of Breed, Westminster 1938.

Ch. Tranquility of Melilotus, outstanding bitch, owned by Mrs.
R. Gilman Smith.

In 1935, Mr. Hunt bought Dunoon Donald Dhu from Andy Dunn in Canada, and did well with him in the States. He was a short well-balanced dog, though large and lacking in angulation.

While resting on his laurels at Green Valley Kennels, his championship certificate hanging on the wall, Donald Dhu took a fancy to our ugly duckling Orientia and, when no one was looking, jumped the fence and bred her. A black male puppy from this litter was sold to William Belleville of Langhorne, Pennsylvania, and was registered "Rodrique of Sandblown Acre". As we shall soon see, Rodrique was to be the first of a line of top winning and producing dogs for this well-known kennel.

Dunoon Donald Dhu was soon sold to Janet Henneberry of Golf, Illinois, who loved him so dearly that she named her kennel for him: "Donnie Dhu."

Fred Hunt brought over another bitch from Mr. Cornthwaite in England named Rufton Rosita, and bred her to Recorder to produce Ch. Green Valley Hercules. Hercules, bred to his half-sister Orientia, produced Tranquillity of Well Sweep, who became the dam of Ch. Tranquillity of Melilotus, Mrs. R. Gilman Smith's outstanding bitch.

Recorder was bred to his granddaughter, Ch. Green Valley Dinah, to produce Ch. Green Valley Oak. Oak, bred to his half-sister, Ch. Green Valley Judy, a Recorder daughter, produced Ch. Green Valley The Feudist.

Recorder was the sire of Ch. Field Marshall, the foundation of Bob Morrow's Audley Farm Kennel, and when linebred through Green Valley Oak, gave Norman Morrow the foundation for his Runor Kennel, Ch. Audley Farm Judy.

Recorder and his offspring are back of Walpride Springers, Rumack, Charlyle, Kaintuck, Wakefield, Inchidony, Frejax, Salilyn and others.

Fred Hunt personally handled Recorder to his championship, as he did most of his Springers. He also ran Green Valley Punch, exclusively, for his Field Trial Championship. Mr. Hunt seldom entered a dog in the Specials class, having little interest in campaigning a dog for Group winning.

In 1941 he was transferred to Detroit, Michigan, so closed Green Valley Kennels. But in a span of ten years, he had finished 56 champions!

Am. & Can. Ch. Rodrique of Sandblown Acre (center) with kennelmates, Ch. Rodrique's Li'le Woodelf, Butterfly of Sandblown Acre, Ch. Riverton Sue and Ch. Rodrique's Li'le Miss Dignity.

A view of Sandblown Acre Kennels, with Rodrique seated on the table in front.

Important Sires Following Recorder

In the wake of Recorder, two sires—above all others—can be credited with leaving their imprint on top-winning Springers of today. They are Am. & Can. Ch. Rodrique of Sandblown Acre and Ch. Inchidony Prince Charming.

Am. & Can. Ch. Rodrique of Sandblown Acre.

AM. & CAN. CH. RODRIQUE OF SANDBLOWN ACRE
(Ch. Dunoon Donald Dhu ex Green Valley Orientia)
Whelped March 12, 1937

Bred at the Green Valley Kennels of Fred Hunt, Rodrique was sold to William Belleville as a puppy. For Mr. Belleville, Rodrique represented an exciting new interest—the dog game. He became the foundation of Sandblown Acre Kennels, named for the Bellevilles' sandy acre of land in Pennsylvania. He was the sire of 28 champions, most of them outstanding producers, including Ch. Co-Pilot of Sandblown Acre with 28 champion get.

Mr. Belleville was the head tomato grower for Campbell Soup Company at the time, and although fairly well along in years and completely inexperienced in dog breeding, bred a good number of winners—all descendants of Rodrique. Unfortunately, this success was short-lived. He found that his theories for breeding bigger, better tomatoes were not applicable to breeding dogs.

Ch. Inchidony Prince Charming ("Charlie").

```
                                          Am. & Can. Ch. Frejax Royal Salute
              Ch. Frejax Royal Request    Frejax Apache Star
        Ch. Salilyn's Sensation           Firebrand of Sandblown Acre, C.D.X.
           Queen Victoria of Salilyn       Salutation of Salilyn
   Ch. Salilyn's Citation II              Firebrand of Sandblown Acre, C.D.X.
           Ch. King Peter of Salilyn       Salutation of Salilyn
        Salilyn's Princess Meg            Ch. Salilyn's Speculation
           Ch. Salilyn's Animation         Salilyn's Lady MacBeth
CH. INCHIDONY PRINCE CHARMING
                                          Traveler of Sandblown Acre
           Firebrand of Sandblown Acre, C.D.X.  Dawn's Elf of Sandblown Acre
        Ch. King Peter of Salilyn         Am. & Can. Ch. Frejax Royal Salute
           Salutation of Salilyn           Nancy of Salilyn
   Ch. Salilyn's Cinderella II            Ch. Co-Pilot of Sandblown Acre
           Ch. Chaltha's The Gainer        Ch. Chaltha's Hope
        Ch. Walpride Gay Beauty           Ch. Dormond's Dark Danger
           Walpride Sensation              Dormond Gypsy
```

Three generations: (*l. to r.*) Ch. Salilyn's Citation II, grandsire; Ch. Inchidony Prince Charming, sire; and two of Prince Charming's sons—Ch. Charlyle's Fair Warning and Ch. Salilyn's Aristocrat.

CH INCHIDONY PRINCE CHARMING
(Ch. Salilyn's Citation II ex Ch. Salilyn's Cinderella II)
Whelped July 8, 1959

Ch. Inchidony Prince Charming was bred by his owners, Becher and Dorothy Hungerford. Mr. Hungerford, a lawyer, is now an American Kennel Club field representative. He and wife Dorothy made "Charlie" a member of their family in a true sense, and he was a constant companion.

Among Prince Charming's 50 champion sons and daughters are the two top winning Springers of their day, Ch. Charlyle's Fair Warning and Ch. Salilyn's Aristocrat, the rocketing littermates—Ch. Canarch Inchidony Sparkler and Ch. Canarch Yankee Patriot, and the National Specialty Best in Show winner, Ch. Ramsgate's Scotch Mist. Interestingly, Prince Charming produced six Best in Show winners out of six different bitches.

It is also interesting that although Prince Charming's sire, Citation, was to win three Bests in Show, 14 Groups, and three Specialties, he had not yet finished his championship when Mr. Hungerford elected to breed Cinderella to him. This was Citation's first mating, and Charlie was the only puppy in the litter!

A lineup of Prince Charming's get. At extreme left is Ch. Salilyn's Aristocrat, and at far right is Ch. Charlyle's Fair Warning.

Both Citation and Cinderella were the result of linebreeding to Rodrique on their paternal *and* maternal sides. Cinderella was a litter sister of Ch. Gay Beauties Academy Award ("Oscar") in a litter of five champions—by Ch. King Peter of Salilyn ex Am. & Can. Ch. Walpride Gay Beauty, whelped July 22, 1956-bred and owned by Thomas A. Blessing. Academy Award was himself the sire of 19 champions, and influential in controlling Springer size in accordance with the 1956 revision of the breed standard.

Ch. Gay Beauties Academy Award—
"Oscar".

```
                Traveler of Sandblown Acre
            Firebrand of Sandblown Acre, C.D.X.
                Dawn's Elf of Sandblown Acre
        Ch. King Peter of Salilyn
                Am. & Can. Ch. Frejax Royal Salute
            Salutation of Salilyn
                Nancy of Salilyn
    AM. & CAN. CH. GAY BEAUTIES ACADEMY AWARD
                Ch. Co-Pilot of Sandblown Acre
            Ch. Chalta's The Gainer
                Ch. Chalta's Hope
        Am. & Can. Ch. Walpride's Gay Beauty
                Ch. Dormond Dark Danger
            Walpride Sensation
                Dormond Gypsy
```

Am. and Can. Ch. Frejax Royal Salute,
with owner Fred Jackson.

	Ch. Rodrique of Sandblown Acre	Ch. Dunoon Donald Dhu
Ch. Co-Pilot of Sandblown Acre		Orientia
	Ch. Rodrique's Li"le Woodelf	Ch. Rodrique of Sandblown Acre
Ch. Sir Lancelot of Salilyn		Bridgewater Countess
	Ch. Rufton Breeze of Rob Roy	Ch. Fleetfoot Dan
Nancy of Salilyn		Frejax Dream Girl
	Ch. Bigenough	Ch. Top Hole of Blighty
		Ch. Highbank Hopeful
AM. & CAN. CH. FREJAX ROYAL SALUTE		Eng. Ch. Advent of Solway
	Ch. Beauchief Outcross	Reece of Solway
Eng. Am. Can. Ch. Showman of Shotton		Eng. Ch. Beauchief Benefactor
	Betty of Highedge	Upperheartsay Betty
Ch. Frejax Lilac Time		Ch. Trent Valley Luckystrike
	Ch. Chancellor of Olmstead	Marol Peggy of Olmstead
Chancellor's Lucky Dignity		Errand Boy of Avandale
	Grasom Bloometta	Virginia of Avandale

13
Ten Modern Greats

THERE HAVE BEEN many notable Springers in the show rings since 1945. From this distinguished number, I have tried here—in view of the limited space—to select the ten that I believe were most outstanding in meeting the two-pronged qualification of having established great show records themselves, and of siring get that were likewise outstanding winners and producers. It is particularly interesting, in studying the pedigrees of the dogs that are dominant in the rings today, to note that almost without exception they stem from these dogs.

The ten, presented in chronological order, are:
Am. & Can. Ch. Frejax Royal Salute
Ch. Melilotus Royal Oak
Ch. King Peter of Salilyn
Am. & Can. Ch. Walpride Flaming Rocket
Am. & Can. Ch. Salilyn's Macduff
Am. & Can. Ch. Waiterock Elmer Brown
Ch. Lee Vee's High Trump
Ch. Wakefield's Black Knight
Ch. Charlyle's Fair Warning
Ch. Salilyn's Aristocrat

Am. & Can. Ch. Frejax Royal Salute and
his sire, Ch. Sir Lancelot of Salilyn.

AM. & CAN. CH. FREJAX ROYAL SALUTE
(liver/white—whelped 1945)

Royal Salute was bred by his owner, Fred Jackson, Frejax Kennels, Oak Park, Michigan—a sincere breeder whose entire adult life was devoted to dogs. Salute established a record of 31 Bests in Show during his lifetime and 55 Group Firsts, and sired 51 champions. He was the first Springer to twice win the Sporting Group at Westminster Kennel Club at Madison Square Garden in New York. His Bests in Show included win of the International at Chicago, and two wins of the Detroit Kennel Club show.

Salute was a descendant of Ch. Rodrique of Sandblown Acre through his sire, Ch. Sir Lancelot, but he himself was an outcross—his dam being a Showman of Shotton daughter. She, Frejax Lilac Time, was a champion, but produced nothing of quality when bred to other sires.

It is of interest to note that Fred Jackson was the first to use Sir Lancelot, then just a ten-months-old puppy and not yet shown, and that father and son later became strong contenders in the ring. Luckily Dad got in three Best in Show wins before Sonny appeared on the scene, after which he was only once the winner.

Fred Jackson bred many other fine dogs. Possibly the best known was Am. & Can. Ch. Frejax Royalist, winner of five Bests in Show including Chicago International. Royalist was "Springer of the Year" in

Am. & Can. Ch. Frejax Royal Request.

1958 and 1959. He was not sired by Royal Salute as most people assume, but rather by Ch. King Peter of Salilyn.

Another outstanding Frejax dog was Am. & Can. Ch. Frejax Royal Request, a striking black-and-white with excellent bone and feet.

Fred Jackson had mastered the art of grooming and handling a Springer. It was a thrilling experience to watch him in the ring with Salute. Man and dog were both magnificent showmen—they performed in complete unison, each giving his "all."

Ch. Frejax Royalist.

CH. MELILOTUS ROYAL OAK
(liver/white—whelped 1949)

```
                    Ch. Co-Pilot of Sandblown Acre
            Ch. Sir Lancelot of Salilyn
                    Nancy of Salilyn
    Am. & Can. Ch. Frejax Royal Salute
                    Eng. & Am. Ch. Showman of Shotton
            Ch. Frejax Lilac Time
                    Chancellor's Lucky Dignity
CH. MELILOTUS ROYAL OAK
                    Ch. Green Valley Oak
            Ch. Gay Skipper
                    Comet
    Ch. Tranquillity of Melilotus
                    Ch. Green Valley Hercules
            Tranquillity of Well Sweep
                    Orientia
```

The famous Melilotus prefix identifies the dogs bred by Mrs. R. Gilman Smith, now Mrs. Frederick Brown. Mrs. Brown, who now lives in the Virgin Islands, still devotes much of her time to Springers as Vice-President and Show Chairman of the parent club, and as a judge, but is no longer actively breeding or showing dogs.

Royal Oak was the winner of the first National Specialty Show in 1956. He was also the first Springer to win Best in Show at the American Spaniel Club Specialty in New York, which he did in 1954, and scored seven all-breed Bests in Show.

Oak sired 33 champions—many of which became top producers themselves—and was Springer Sire of the Year for 1957 and 1958.

He was grandsire, on the maternal side, of the Westminster Best in Show—Ch. Wakefield's Black Knight. Oak was linebred, although not immediately, to Rufton Recorder. His sire, Royal Salute, was the grandson of Co-Pilot, a Rufton Recorder grandson (Rodrique bred to his daughter). His dam, Tranquillity of Melilotus (dam of 14 champions), was a great granddaughter of Rufton Recorder, and her dam in turn—Tranquillity of Well Sweep—was a Recorder *double* granddaughter.

Ch. Melilotus Royal Oak winning the first National Specialty of the parent English Springer Spaniel Field Trial Association in 1956 under judge Thomas G. Lenfestey. Handler, Ruth Williams. Presenting the trophy is author Mrs. F. H. Gasow.

CH. KING PETER OF SALILYN
(liver/white—whelped 1949)

```
                                                    Ch. Co-Pilot of Sandblown Acre
            G. I. Jack of Sandblown Acre           Ch. Riverton Sue
      Traveler of Sandblown Acre                    Ch. Rodrique of Sandblown Acre
         Eldgyth Cordelia                           Eldgyth Empress
   Firebrand of Sandblown Acre, C.D.X.              Am. & Can. Ch. Dunoon Donald Dhu
         Ch. Rodrique of Sandblown Acre             Orientia
      Dawn's Elf of Sandblown Acre                  Ch. Rodrique of Sandblown Acre
         Ch. Rodrique's Li'le Woodelf               Bridgewater Countess
CH. KING PETER OF SALILYN                           Ch. Co-Pilot of Sandblown Acre
         Ch. Sir Lancelot of Salilyn                Nancy of Salilyn
      Am. & Can. Ch. Frejax Royal Salute            Eng. Am. Can. Ch. Showman of Shotton
         Ch. Frejax Lilac Time                      Chancellor's Lucky Dignity
   Salutation of Salilyn                            Ch. Fleetfoot Dan
         Ch. Rufton Breeze of Rob Roy               Frejax Dream Girl
      Nancy of Salilyn                              Ch. Frejax Top Hole of Blighty
         Ch. Bigenough                              Ch. Highbank Hopeful
```

King Peter was bred by our Salilyn Kennels at Troy, Michigan. His record included 22 Bests in Show, 6 Specialties, and 36 Group Firsts, and he sired 35 champions.

Before 1956 the Parent Club did not make annual awards as it does today. Instead, it presented a beautiful sterling silver trophy for Best of Breed at designated Specialty Shows. Peter won this trophy in 1951, 1952, and 1953.

He received the Ken-L Ration Midwestern Division award for 1954, awarded to the dog (of any breed) having the most Group Firsts in the division for the year. Peter was the first Springer to win Best of Breed at Westminster three times, which he did in 1951, 1954, and 1955, and won the Group there in 1955.

Peter was linebred on both sides to Rodrique. And while neither his sire nor his dam were champions, both were of great importance to the breed. Sire Firebrand represented a concentration of Rodrique, and therefore Recorder, bloodlines. Mr. Belleville had heavily inbred to produce this dog. Firebrand's dam was the result of breeding Rodrique to Rodrique's daughter. His great grandsire, Ch. Co-Pilot of Sandblown Acre, was a combination of the same son and daughter. As a matter of fact, there are three father (Rodrique) to daughter matings in "Brandy's" pedigree.

```
                        Ch. Co-Pilot of Sandblown Acre
                 G. I. Jack of Sandblown Acre
                        Ch. Riverton Sue
              Traveler of Sandblown Acre
                        Ch. Rodrique of Sandblown Acre
                 Eldgyth Cordelia
                        Eldgyth Empress
          FIREBRAND OF SANDBLOWN ACRE, C.D.X.
                        Am. & Can. Ch. Dunoon Donald Dhu
                 Ch. Rodrique of Sandblown Acre
                        Orientia
              Dawn's Elf of Sandblown Acre
                        Ch. Rodrique of Sandblown Acre
                 Ch. Rodrique's Li'le Woodelf
                        Bridgewater Countess
```

Firebrand was not a good show specimen. He did acquire 23 championship points, but never a "major". Because of his unimpressive appearance, he was seldom used at stud, but in such progeny as Peter proved himself. "Brandy's" C.D.X. gives just a hint of his brilliance. He truly thought as people think and seemed to understand one's every move. And he had the greatest temperament I have yet to find in any dog.

Peter's dam, Salutation, was the result of breeding Nancy of Salilyn to her grandson, Frejax Royal Salute. Bred only to Firebrand, she was

Firebrand of Sandblown Acre, C.D.X.
"Brandy"

the mother of eight champions—four of them Best in Show winners. Of these, Ch. King William of Salilyn had a record surpassed only by that of King Peter. Though in competition with his more illustrious elder brother, William won five Bests in Show, many Group Firsts, and produced well-known champion sons and daughters including the record-breaking Salilyn's Macduff.

Ch. King William of Salilyn.

AM. & CAN. CH. WALPRIDE FLAMING ROCKET
(black/white—whelped 1950)

```
                Am. & Can. Ch. Rodrique of Sandblown Acre    Am. & Can. Ch. Dunoon Donald Dhu
       Ch. Co-Pilot of Sandblown Acre                        Orientia
              Ch. Rodrique's Li'le Woodelf                   Ch. Rodrique of Sandblown Acre
   Ch. Chaltha's The Gainer                                  Bridgewater Countess
              Ch. Rufton Breeze of Rob Roy                   Ch. Fleetfoot Dan
       Ch. Chaltha's Hope                                    Frejax Dream Girl
              Ch. Victoria Carlotta                          His Nibs of Gamelyn
                                                             Miss Tranquil of Ten Broeck
AM. & CAN. CH. WALPRIDE FLAMING ROCKET
              Ch. Sir Lancelot of Salilyn                    Ch. Co-Pilot of Sandblown Acre
       Dormond Dark Danger                                   Nancy of Salilyn
              Dormond Gypsy                                  Ch. Rufton Breeze of Rob Roy
   Walpride Sensation                                        Grandyle Beauty
              Ch. Rufton Breeze of Rob Roy                   Ch. Fleetfoot Dan
       Dormond Gypsy                                         Frejax Dream Girl
              Grandyle Beauty                                Tops O Day
                                                             Kay T.B.
```

Rocket was bred by Robert J. Walgate, Walpride Kennels, Clarence, N.Y. Mr. Walgate is a professional handler, licensed to handle all

Ch. Walpride Country Squire, 1/w, winning Best in Show at
Buffalo, 1966. Judge, Dr. Wilfred Shute. Owner-handler, Robert J.
Walgate of Clarence, N.Y.

breeds. This has many times prevented him from showing his own
Springers, since his clients' dogs have been given first consideration. In
spite of the handicap, Rocket was a top Best in Show and Group winner, and became the sire of 42 champions.

This handsome dog is the foundation of Beryltown Kennels, one of
the leading show and producing kennels of today, and was a litter
brother of Am. & Can. Ch. Walpride Gay Beauty, the foundation of
Thomas Blessing's famous Gay Beauties Kennels. Rocket was linebred
to Rodrique through Ch. Co-Pilot of Sandblown Acre.

Am. & Can. Ch. Walpride Sandeman had earlier made a name for
Bob Walgate. Sandeman was sired by Rodrique out of Woodelf Gypsy
of Hampton, a great granddaughter of Rufton Recorder on both her
paternal and maternal sides. In more recent years, the many times Best
in Show winner, Ch. Walpride Country Squire, has brought new pride
for Walpride homebreds.

Am. & Can. Ch. Walpride Sandeman.

Ch. Beryltown Bold Crusader, 1/w, a grandson of Rocket on both sides of his pedigree (see Page 234). "Dusty" won his first all-breed Best in Show in 1966, and then in 1967 added two more and topped the national Specialty. Bred by Beryl Hines, and owned by Earl Taisey of Rockville, Maryland. Handled by Bobby Barlow.

Am. & Can. Ch. Salilyn's Macduff.

AM. & CAN. CH. SALILYN'S MACDUFF
(liver/white—whelped 1954)

```
            Traveler of Sandblown Acre         G. I. Jack of Sandblown Acre
    Firebrand of Sandblown Acre, C.D.X.        Eldgyth Cordelia
        Dawn's Elf of Sandblown Acre           Ch. Rodrique of Sandblown Acre
Ch. King William of Salilyn                    Ch. Rodrique's Li'le Woodelf
    Am. & Can. Ch. Frejax Royal Salute         Ch. Sir Lancelot of Salilyn
    Salutation of Salilyn                      Ch. Frejax Lilac Time
    Nancy of Salilyn                           Ch. Rufton Breeze of Rob Roy
                                               Ch. Bigenough
AM. & CAN. CH. SALILYN'S MACDUFF               Ch. Rodrique of Sandblown Acre
        Ch. Co-Pilot of Sandblown Acre         Ch. Rodrique's Li'le Woodelf
    Ch. Sir Lancelot of Salilyn                Ch. Rufton Breeze of Rob Roy
    Nancy of Salilyn                           Ch. Bigenough
Shercliff's Lady Debby                         Ch. Rufton Breeze of Rob Roy
    Rufton of Lawlands                         Ch. Upyonder Janny
    Candy Kisses of Kanona                     Pride n' Joy of Astabrook
    Princess Sue Ann of Kanona                 Ladybelle of Duckerbird
```

In 1959, Macduff became the top show winning Springer to that time. His 39 Best in Show wins and 81 Group Firsts surpassed the record of Am. & Can. Ch. Frejax Royal Salute, and stood as the mark until the achievements of Ch. Salilyn's Aristocrat and then Ch. Chinoe's Adamant James, a decade later.

Macduff was bred by Robert E. Gibson and James E. Mitchell. He was originally owned by the author, and later, having won 5 Bests in Show and the Ken-L Ration Award for 1957 with 31 Group Firsts, was sold to William L. and Elaine P. Randall. He again won the Ken-L Award for 1958.

Macduff was Best in Show at the National Specialty in 1959, and his record that year placed him second as a show dog of all dogs in the country. He received the Parent Club award for "Springer of the Year" three times—1958, 1959 and 1960.

Because of the tight campaign schedule, Macduff was used only infrequently at stud during his show career. But the champions he did produce are important to us. One is Ch. Salilyn's Inchidony Banquo, winner of 3 Bests in Show and 20 Sporting Groups, and the sire of 10 champions. Four of Banquo's offspring have taken National Specialty points, and current Best in Show and Group winner, Ch. Canarch Juniper Five, is a Banquo son.

Am. and Can. Ch. Waiterock Elmer Brown, at 10 years of age, with his owner, Mrs. Juanita Waite Howard of Lafayette, California.

AM. & CAN. CH. WAITEROCK ELMER BROWN
(liver/white—whelped 1956)

```
                Elf's Sportsman of Breeze
        Ch. Waiterock Strongbow
                Timpanagos Showman's Peg
    Ch. Waiterock Whistle
                Am. & Can. Ch. Clipfort Press Agent
        Woodelf of Meadowgrove
                Fast Brunette of Breeze
AM. & CAN. CH. WAITEROCK ELMER BROWN
                Ch. Green Valley the Feudist
        Ch. Sensation of Caulier's
                Caulier's Royal Maggie
    Tahquitz Merry Mischief
                Ch. Tahquitz El Don
        Tahquitz Fastepper
                Frejax Hi-Stepper
```

Elmer was bred and owned by Juanita Waite Howard, of Waiterock Ranch, Lafayette, California. An outstanding winner and producer on the West Coast, he was honored as Best Western Sporting Dog in 1962, 1963 and 1964. He was the parent club "Springer of the Year" in 1964, and the top winning Springer in the Phillips System ratings for 1962, 1963 and 1964. Elmer's wins included 8 Bests in Show, 44 Sporting Groups and 187 Bests of Breed (including 16 Specialties). It is interesting that two of Elmer's Specialty wins were from the Veteran's Class, at Beverly Hills and Richmond, California, at the age of eleven years!

Elmer was "Top Springer Sire of the Year" for 1964, 1965, 1966 and 1967. He was sire of more than twenty champions, and one of his litters alone produced seven champions.

CH. LEE VEE'S HIGH TRUMP
(liver/white—whelped 1957)

```
                    Can. Ch. Keith's Brownie
              Ch. Kay's Chico
                    Butterfly of Burnside
        Ch. Carpenter's Diamond Wings, C.D.X.
                    Ch. Kay's Popcorn Cavalier
              Carpenter's Diamond Lil
                    Ouabache Gilded Maiden
  CH. LEE VEE'S HIGH TRUMP
                    Firebrand of Sandblown Acre, C.D.X.
              Ch. Salilyn's King Arthur
                    Salutation of Salilyn
        Ch. Sir Kay's Black Satin, C.D.
                    Ch. Frejax Firebrand Fluff
              Ch. Bo-Kare Stormy Sal, C.D.
                    Thirty Acres' Roxy
```

High Trump was bred and owned by Vivian Diffendaffer, a lawyer of Oklahoma City. It is largely through the efforts and enthusiasm of Mrs. Diffendaffer that interest in Springers is high in Texas and surrounding states, a considerable accomplishment in view of the great distances between Springer owners in that part of the country. Mrs. Diffendaffer has always found time to help Springer owners groom and show their dogs, and has frequently handled dogs for friends in the ring.

High Trump was a top winner and producer in the area. He had over 10 Bests in Show and 40 Groups, and was the parent club's "Springer of the Year" twice—in 1960 and 1961. "Sire of the Year" for 1963, he stands as sire of more than 50 champions.

Most outstanding of High Trump's progeny has been Ch. Debonair Dandy, winner of the National Specialty in 1964 and the parent club "Springer of the Year" for 1965 with winning that included the breed at Westminster and at Chicago International.

Ch. Lee Vee's High Trump, with breeder-owner
Mrs. Vivian Diffendaffer of Oklahoma City.

Ch. Salilyn's Inchidony Banquo, whelped 1961, son of Macduff.

Ch. Debonair Dandy, High Trump's son, winning Best of Breed at Westminster 1965 under judge Reed Hankwitz. Owner, Vivian Diffendaffer. Handler, Jack Funk.

CH. WAKEFIELD'S BLACK KNIGHT
(black/white—whelped 1959)

Ch. Wakefield's Black Knight, or "Danny", was bred by Mrs. W. J. S. Borie, Gwynedd Valley, Pennsylvania, and loved by all who knew

Three generations: At left is Ch. Wakefield's Black Knight; in center, his sire, Ch. Kaintuck Christmas Carol; and, at right, his grandsire, Ch. Kaintuck Beau Brummel.

```
                    Beau Geste of Sandblown Acre
             Ch. Kaintuck Beau Brummel
                    Kaintuck Roxane
        Ch. Kaintuck Christmas Carol
                    Ch. Frejax Prince Peter
             Ch. Cartref Spring Chime
                    Cartref Cae of Bittersweet
CH. WAKEFIELD'S BLACK KNIGHT
                    Am. & Can. Ch. Frejax Royal Salute
             Ch. Melilotus Royal Oak
                    Ch. Tranquillity of Melilotus
        Ch. Wakefield's Fanny
                    Ch. Runor's Deacon
             Judy of Gwynedd
                    Victoria of Gwynedd
```

him. He lived only five years, but in that time scored 7 Bests in Show
and 24 Group Firsts, and was the sire of numerous champions.

"Danny" will always be remembered as the first English Springer
Spaniel to have won Best in Show at Westminster, a glory he achieved
in 1963. In addition, he was the first Springer to twice win the National
Specialty—1961 and 1963.

Black Knight traced back to Rodrique on both sides. Rodrique is
four generations back of Kaintuck Christmas Carol, Danny's sire, and
Danny's dam, Wakefield's Fanny, was sired by Ch. Melilotus Royal
Oak.

Ch. Kaintuck Christmas Carol, sire of Ch. Wakefield's Black Knight.

CH. CHARLYLE'S FAIR WARNING
(black/white—whelped 1962)

Charlyle's Fair Warning was bred by Charles R. Clement, who handled him to his championship and then sold him to Ann Pope of Boston. "Sam" has established himself as winner and sire of winners. His show score includes 4 Bests in Show, 9 independent Specialties and 43 Group

```
                    Ch. Salilyn's Sensation, C.D.
           Am. & Can. Ch. Salilyn's Citation II
                    Salilyn's Princess Meg
       Ch. Inchidony Prince Charming
                    Ch. King Peter of Salilyn
           Ch. Salilyn's Cinderella II
                    Am. & Can. Ch. Walpride Gay Beauty
CH. CHARLYLE'S FAIR WARNING
                    Ch. Ebony of Hillcrest
           Ch. Banneret's Regal Brigadier
                    Banneret's Gay Festival
     Charlyle's Nanette
                    Salilyn's Young Lochinvar
     Charlyle's Happy Choice
                    Ch. Charlyle's Royal Heiress
```

Firsts. He won the National Specialty in 1966 and the parent club award for "Springer of the Year" for 1966 and 1968. And to date, he's the sire of 23 champions.

Sam is but one of the many fine Springers that have come from the Charlyle Kennels, named for Charlie Clement and his wife, Lyle. Starting in 1933 with a roan tri-colored bitch, their success really began with the breeding of a granddaughter of Ch. Co-Pilot of Sandblown Acre to Ch. Frejax Royal Minstrel, a breeding that gave them the excellent producer—Ch. Charlyle's Royal Flush.

Among many proud moments for the kennel, a highlight has to be the win of the National Specialty in 1962 by Charlyle's Holdout, from the Open class: Holdout was bred, owned and handled by Mr. Clement.

Ch. Charlyle's Royal Flush.

Charlyle's Nanette, dam of Ch. Charlyle's Fair Warning.

Ch. Charlyle's Eroica, Dam of the Year for 1967, dam of four champions in one litter.

Ch. Charlyle's Holdout.

CH. SALILYN'S ARISTOCRAT
(liver/white—whelped 1964)

```
                                              Ch. Frejax Royal Request
        Ch. Salilyn's Sensation, C.D.         Queen Victoria of Salilyn
    Am. & Can. Ch. Salilyn's Citation II      Ch. King Peter of Salilyn
        Salilyn's Princess Meg                Ch. Salilyn's Animation II
Ch. Inchidony Prince Charming                 Firebrand of Sandblown Acre, C.D.X.
        Ch. King Peter of Salilyn             Salutation of Salilyn
    Ch. Salilyn's Cinderella II               Ch. Chaltha's The Gainer
        Am. & Can. Ch. Walpride Gay Beauty    Walpride Sensation

CH. SALILYN'S ARISTOCRAT                      Ch. Salilyn's Sensation, C.D.
    .  Am. & Can. Ch. Salilyn's Citation II   Salilyn's Princess Meg
        Salilyn's Royal Consort               Ch. Ascot's Ajax
        Ch. Ascot's Estralita                 Ascot's Diamond Lil
    Ch. Salilyn's Lily of the Valley          Firebrand of Sandblown Acre, C.D.X.
        Ch. King William of Salilyn           Salutation of Salilyn
        Salilyn's Glenda                      Ch. Cartref Bob Bobbin
        Ch. Salilyn's Good Omen               Salilyn's Surprise
```

In the calendar year of 1967, before he had reached his third birthday, Ch. Salilyn's Aristocrat won a total of 45 Bests in Show and 71 Group Firsts to establish an all-time record for all breeds—a Phillips Rating total of 34,553 points for the year! This record stood just until 1971 when—in what must be the ultimate honor for any serious dog breeder—it was surpassed by Aristocrat's son, Ch. Chinoe's Adamant James. (See Page 212).

Following his record-breaking year, Risto was removed from regular competition by his breeder-owner, Mrs. Julia Gasow, and has been shown just four times since: at Westminster in 1968, where he placed second in the Sporting Group; at the annual National Specialty Shows in 1968 and 1969, where he was Best in Show each time; and then, at age of eight, again at Westminster 1973, where he spectacularly won the breed and third in the Group.

Risto's winning had gotten off to an early start. He finished his championship at nine months of age from the Puppy Class, and from this class won his first Group. In all, he has won 66 Bests in Show, 108 Sporting Groups and 5 Specialty Shows including Best in Show at the American Spaniel Club Specialty in 1967. He was winner of both the Ken-L Rations Award and the parent club "Springer of the Year" in 1967.

But outstanding as he has been as a winner, it is as a producer that Ch. Salilyn's Aristocrat will be richest remembered. As already noted,

Ch. Salilyn's Aristocrat.

Ch. Salilyn's Lily of the Valley, dam of Ch. Salilyn's Aristocrat. Handled here by Ruth Cooper.

his son Ch. Chinoe's Adamant James became the greatest winning show dog in American canine history in 1971. Another son, Ch. Salilyn's Colonel's Overlord, also a many-time Best in Show and Group winner, was the top winning Springer of 1969 and second only to Adamant James in 1970. At this printing, Aristocrat is already the sire of 85 champions, and is one of but four dogs (the others: Ch. Chik T'Sun of Caversham, a Pekingese; Ch. Bang Away of Sirrah Crest, a Boxer; and Ch. Shirkhan of Grandeur, an Afghan Hound) enshrined in the Kennel Review Hall of Fame.

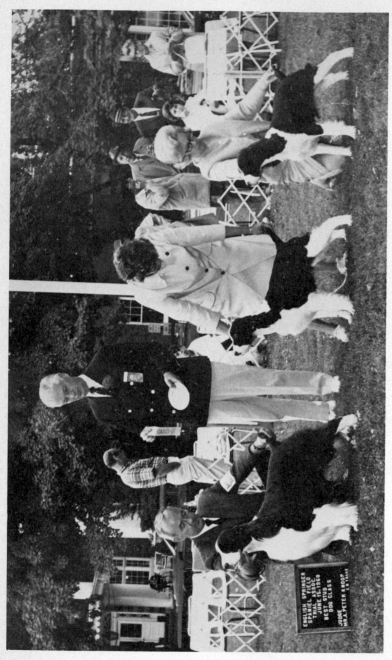

Ch. Salilyn's Aristocrat, following upon his win of Best of Breed at the 1968 national ESSFTA Specialty, is pictured winning the Stud Dog class at the same show under judge Peter Knoop. Risto, at left, is followed by his son, Salilyn's Colonel Overlord (winner of the Puppy Dog 6–9 months class) and his daughter, Salilyn's Sophistication (winner of the Puppy Bitch 6–9 months class). These littermates are now outstanding champions.

14
Important Springer Bitches

A DOG and a bitch each has its place in a show kennel's breeding program, but for many the possession of a good bitch is the more important requirement. This is based on the realization that one may breed to the top-winning dog in the country without owning him. "A kennel is no better than its bitches" bears remembering.

Still, for winning show dogs we must stay with the males. The soft temperament of the Springer female is no match for the flashy, aggressive male in the ring.

Famous producing bitches well merit a book devoted specifically to them, and to the importance of their get. However, here we must limit ourselves, so we have selected five whose progeny among current winners have particularly distinguished them. For added study, we include their pedigrees.

CH. CARTREF DONLA'S ARPEGE, C.D.
(liver/white—whelped 1959)
Breeder: Doris Haverstick
Owner: Beryl Hines, Alexandria, Va.

Arpege's 9 champion offspring include winners of a National Specialty, of many other Specialty Shows, and of an all-breed Best in Show.

```
                    Ch. Sir Lancelot of Salilyn          Ch. Co-Pilot of Sandblown Acre
        Am. & Can. Ch. Frejax Royal Salute               Nancy of Salilyn
                    Ch. Frejax Lilac Time                Eng. Am. Can. Ch. Showman of Shotton
        Ch. Prince Charlie of Melilotus                  Chancellor's Lucky Dignity
                    Ch. Gay Skipper                      Ch. Green Valley Oak
            Ch. Tranquillity of Melilotus               Comet
                    Tranquillity of Well Sweep           Ch. Green Valley Hercules
CH. CARTREF DONLA'S ARPEGE, C.D.                         Orientia
                                                         Firebrand of Sandblown Acre, C.D.X.
                    Ch. King Peter of Salilyn            Salutation of Salilyn
            Ch. Cartref Wizard                           Ch. Sir Lancelot of Salilyn
                    Lady Millicent of Salilyn            Miss Clover of Sandblown Acre
        Ch. Cartref Tali Hi                              Am. & Can. Ch. Frejax Royal Salute
                    Am. & Can. Ch. Frejax Royal Minstrel Tittabawassee Dusky Iz
            Ch. Cartref Chimneysweep                     Ch. Rodrique of Sandblown Acre
                    Ch. Chatterbox of Sandblown Acre     Betsy B. of Sandblown Acre
```

CH. PHYLISS DUCHESS OF PEMBROKE, C.D.
(black/white—whelped 1963)
Breeder-Owner: Alice Berd, Birmingham, Mich.

Phyliss is dam of 5 champions, including the Winners Dog and Winners Bitch at the 1966 National Specialty Show, the only littermates to have achieved this sweep. She is also the dam of the 1967 and 1968 National Futurity winners, and of the 1968 Winners Bitch. Her son, Ch. Pembroke Inchidony Scot, C.D. had 7 Bests in Show in 1971, and was second only to Ch. Chinoe's Adamant James for Phillips honors in that year.

```
                  Firebrand of Sandblown Acre, C.D.X.
          Ch. King Peter of Salilyn
              Salutation of Salilyn
      Ch. Salilyn's Santa Claus
              Ch. Sunhi's Christmas Star
          Ch. Salilyn's Evening Star
              Salilyn's Surprise
  CH. PHYLISS DUCHESS OF PEMBROKE, C.D.
              Am. & Can. Ch. Frejax Royal Request
          Ch. Salilyn's Sensation, C.D.
              Queen Victoria of Salilyn
      Grande Pointe's First Lady
              Ch. King Peter of Salilyn
          Ch. Gay Beauties Princess Pat, C.D.
              Am. & Can. Ch. Walpride Gay Beauty
```

CH. CANARCH INCHIDONY BROOK
(black/white—whelped 1964)
Breeder: Charles Hendee
Owner: Ann Roberts, Lexington, Ky.

Brook's 5 champion sons include the all-time
record setter for the breed and two-time Best
in Show winner at Westminster, Ch. Chinoe's
Adamant James, and Best in Show winner Ch.
Canarch Juniper Five.

```
              Ch. Salilyn's Sensation, C.D.
       Am. & Can. Ch. Salilyn's Citation II
              Salilyn's Princess Meg
    Ch. Inchidony Prince Charming
              Ch. King Peter of Salilyn
       Ch. Salilyn's Cinderella II
              Am. & Can. Ch. Walpride Gay Beauty

CH. CANARCH INCHIDONY BROOK
              Ch. Kaintuck Marc Anthony
       Ch. Syringa Disc Jockey
              Ch. Syringa Sue
    Ch. Canarch Sunnyside, C.D.
              Ch. Rostherne Hunter
       Melilotus Hufty Tufty
              Melilotus Princess Dona
```

CH. SALILYN'S RADIANCE
(black/white—whelped 1966)
Breeder: Mrs. F. H. Gasow
Owner: Col. Forrest Andrews, Colorado Springs, Colo.

"Glory" is dam of the outstanding duo—Ch. Salilyn's Colonel Overlord, Springer of the Year for 1969 and a consistent winner since, and his Group-winning sister, Ch. Salilyn's Sophistication.

```
                                              Ch. King William of Salilyn
                   Ch. Salilyn's Macduff      Shercliffe's Lady Debbie
            Ch. Salilyn's Cocktail Time       Ch. King Peter of Salilyn
                   Ch. Salilyn's Concerto      Ch. Ascot's Estralita
         Salilyn's Good Fortune               Ch. Cartref Talisman
                   Ch. Cartref Bob Bobbin     Cartref Fire of Bittersweet
            Ch. Salilyn's Good Omen           Ch. Salilyn's Sensation, C.D.
                   Salilyn's Surprise         Salutation of Salilyn

   CH. SALILYN'S RADIANCE                     Firebrand of Sandblown Acre, C.D.X.
                   Ch. King William of Salilyn  Salutation of Salilyn
            Ch. Salilyn's Macduff             Ch. Sir Lancelot of Salilyn
                   Shercliffe's Lady Debbie    Candy Kisses of Kanona
         Ch. Randalane's Bright Chips         Ch. Kaintuck Prince Hamlet
                   Ch. Kaintuck Marc Anthony   Kaintuck Roxanne
            Ch. Ascot's Libby                 Ch. Sunhi's Christmas Star
                   Ch. Sunhi's Doody          Sunhi's Duchess
```

AM. & CAN. CH. NOBILITY'S VENETIAN DAWN, AM. & CAN. U.D.

(whelped 1965)
Breeder: George Kitto
Owned and trained by Marjorie and Gilbert Rollins

Dawn was winner of the Kennel Review Top Producers Award in 1970 and 1972. She is dam of 8 American champions, all of which have Obedience degrees. Seven of these are also Canadian champions, one with C.D. degree. Her daughter, Am. & Can. Ch. S. Cricket Venetian, C.D. received the Kennel Review award in 1971, a second-generation Top Producer. Her son, Am. & Can. Ch. Venetian Count Casanova, Am. & Can. C.D., was No. 5 Springer in the United States in 1972, and No. 2 in Canada.

```
                                              Firebrand of Sandblown Acre, C.D.X.
            Ch. King William of Salilyn       Salutation of Salilyn
        Ch. Salilyn's Macduff                 Ch. Sir Lancelot of Salilyn
            Shercliff's Lady Debbie            Candy Kisses of Kanona
    Ch. Salilyn's Cocktail Time               Firebrand of Sandblown Acre, C.D.X.
            Ch. King Peter of Salilyn          Salutation of Salilyn
        Ch. Salilyn's Concerto                 Ch. Ascot's Ajax
            Ch. Ascot's Estralita              Ascot's Diamond Lil
CH. NOBILITY VENETIAN DAWN
                                              Ch. Salilyn's Sensation, C.D.
            Ch. Salilyn's Citation II          Salilyn's Princess Meg
        Salilyn's Royal Consort                Ch. Ascot's Ajax
            Ch. Ascot's Estralita              Ascot's Diamond Lil
    Ch. Salilyn's Nobility Rose               Firebrand of Sandblown Acre, C.D.X.
            Ch. King William of Salilyn        Salutation of Salilyn
        Salilyn's Glenda                       Ch. Cartref Bob Bobbin
            Ch. Salilyn's Good Omen            Salilyn's Surprise
```

Ch. Schwedekrest Sensation, twice honored as "Bitch of the Year". A Best of Breed and Group winner, bred and owned by Lucille Schwede of Midway, Washington.

Ch. El Rey's Reina of Whitney, 1972 parent club "Bitch of the Year". "Lola", bred by Alta V. Pleasant, is the daughter of Aristocrat ex Ch. Anglodale's Mocha Amulet, and is owned by Eli and Frances Franco of Whittier, California.

15
Later English Imports

THERE HAVE BEEN comparatively few English Springer Spaniel show dogs brought over from England since 1949. Those having the most influence on current Springers were imported by Mrs. R. Gilman Smith (now Mrs. Frederick Brown) of Melilotus Kennels, and by Mr. W. E. MacKinney of Mac Mar Kennels.

In 1959, on one of several trips that she had made to England, Mrs. Smith acquired Ch. Rostherne Hunter. He stands as the most important import in the last two decades, and was used most effectively at stud in the East. However, today, more of his get and their offspring appear in winning circles through the efforts of a Midwestern breeder—Henriette Schmidt of Brookfield, Wisconsin.

Mr. MacKinney's goal has always been to breed show dogs that are qualified hunters as well. His first purchase from England, in 1959, comprised five Springers, bought for the distinct purpose of breed improvement. Although Mac Mar Kennels (of Elgin, Illinois) had been established since 1934, the English importations marked the beginning of a completely new breeding program. The best producers of the imports were Ch. Studley Grenadier of Stubham and Eng. Ch. Sheilah of Stubham. A combination of the two produced Ch. Mac Mar's Philip, W.D.X., and Philip in turn was the sire of another fine winner, Ch. Mac Mar's Midnight Spark, W.D.X.

CH. ROSTHERNE HUNTER, W.D.
(liver—whelped December 17, 1957)
By Ch. Studley Major ex Ch. Rostherne Beauty
Breeder: J. Malarkey
Imported and Owned by Mrs. R. Gilman Smith

Ch. Kennersleigh Cleavehill Beliza Bee, b/w, whelped 1966, the first English import bitch to win her championship since the mid-40s, and now established as an important influence with many American champion offspring. Owned by A. Wesley Davis of Salt Lake City, and leased to Mary J. Hosteny of Lafayette, California.

Ch. Studley Grenadier of Stubham, imported from England
by W. E. MacKinney.

Grenadier's son, Ch. Mac Mar
Philip, W.D.X., owned by
Mr. MacKinney.

Philip's son, Ch. Mac
Mar's Midnight Spark,
W.D.X., also owned by
Mr. MacKinney.

The Ch. Rostherne Hunter influence is today seen strongest in the Hillcrest dogs bred and owned by Henriette Schmidt of Brookfield, Wisconsin. At top left is Ch. Gingerbread Gal of Hillcrest, C.D.; at top right, Ch. Gingerbread Boy of Hillcrest, C.D.; and below left, Ch. Amanda Hunter of Hillcrest. All three are by Ch. Rostherne Hunter, W.D. ex Ch. Ginger Snap of Hillcrest. The dog at lower right is Ch. Pied Pedro of Hillcrest, by Ch. Crooked Pine's Black Jack ex Ch. Amanda Hunter of Hillcrest. Most of Mrs. Schmidt's dogs are owner-groomed and handled. She is to be commended not only for the skillful presentation of her own dogs, but for her graciousness in helping other exhibitors and her work to promote the breed.

16

A Pictorial Gallery of Some Notable Recent Springers

Oɴ ᴛʜᴇ ᴘᴀɢᴇs that follow are pictured, together with brief note of their winning or producing records, some of the more prominent winning Springers of recent years. On accompanying pages you will find the pedigrees of many of these dogs. They should prove an interesting and helpful guide to novices establishing themselves in the show sport.

It is only appropriate, however, that we lead off these pages with the winner who stands out above all the rest. While it is too soon to measure Ch. Chinoe's Adamant James as a contributing sire for the breed, his place as a record-breaker assures him immortality.

Ch. Chinoe's Adamant James
"D.J."

CH. CHINOE'S ADAMANT JAMES
(liver/white—whelped 1968)

```
                    Am. & Can. Ch. Salilyn's Citation II
              Ch. Inchidony Prince Charming
                    Ch. Salilyn's Cinderella II
         Ch. Salilyn's Aristocrat
                    Salilyn's Royal Consort
              Ch. Salilyn's Lilly of the Valley
                    Salilyn's Glenda
   CH. CHINOE'S ADAMANT JAMES
                    Am. & Can. Ch. Salilyn's Citation II
              Ch. Inchidony Prince Charming
                    Ch. Salilyn's Cinderella II
         Ch. Canarch Inchidony Brook
                    Ch. Syringa Disc Jockey
              Ch. Canarch Sunnyside, C.D.
                    Melilotus Hufty Tufty
```

In according him his win of Best in Show all-breeds at Westminster in 1971, the late judge O. C. Harriman dubbed Ch. Chinoe's Adamant James "super dog". The accolade seems no exaggeration. "D-J" (derived from his original nickname of Diamond Jim, which he acquired because of a white spot on his hip) stands today with the greatest record of Bests in Show and Group Firsts ever scored by an American show dog within one year—48 Bests in Show and 86 Group Firsts in 1971. Included in this winning were such major events as Westminster, Chicago, Beverly Hills, Indianapolis, Western Reserve, Harrisburg, and a phenomenal streak of 30 consecutive Group Firsts.

Following his spectacular year, "D-J" was shown just three times in 1972, going Best in Show each time: first at the American Spaniel Club, then at Westminster in Madison Square Garden, where he became the first dog in two decades to win Best in Show back-to-back; and then in closing, his home town show at Louisville, Kentucky. This brought his career total to 61 Bests in Show, 107 Groups, and 3 Specialties.

Adamant James was bred by Mrs. Ann Roberts of Lexington, Kentucky. Whelped June 30, 1968, he was purchased at the age of only ten weeks by the family of Dr. Milton E. Prickett, a Lexington veterinarian, as a birthday gift for Dr. Prickett (who had designated his choice of the litter two weeks earlier). "D-J" was shown throughout his career by Mrs. Roberts' brother, professional handler Clint Harris.

LAKE SHORE
KENNEL CLUB
APRIL 21,1968
FIRST IN
SPORTING GROUP
Photo by Ritter

Ch. Canarch Juniper Five, 1/w, whelped 1966. Always a dependable showman, Juniper is winner of Bests in Show, Specialties, and many Groups. Sire of Best in Show winning get. Bred by Charles Hendee, and owned by Ann H. Roberts of Lexington, Ky.

```
                        Ch. King William of Salilyn
            Ch. Salilyn's MacDuff
                        Shercliffe's Lady Debbie
        Ch. Salilyn's Inchidony Banquo
                        Ch. King Peter of Salilyn
            Ch. Salilyn's Cinderella II
                        Am. & Can. Ch. Walpride Gay Beauty

    CH. CANARCH JUNIPER FIVE
                        Ch. Salilyn's Citation II
            Ch. Inchidony Prince Charming
                        Ch. Salilyn's Cinderella II
        Ch. Canarch Inchidony Brook
                        Ch. Syringa Disc Jockey
            Ch. Canarch Sunnyside, C.D.
                        Melilotus Hufty Tufty
```

Ch. Salilyn Colonel's Overlord, (b/w, whelped 1967), winner of the parent club award as Springer of the Year for 1969. Also the top Phillips System winner in the breed, and the only Springer to place in the Top Ten Sporting in that year. "Andy", bred by Col. Forrest Andrews of Colorado Springs, is co-owned by Col. Andrews and Mrs. Julia Gasow. Handled by Dick Cooper.

Ch. Salilyn's Sophistication, 1/w, a litter sister of Colonel's Overlord, bred by Col. Forrest Andrews and owned by Mrs. Julia Gasow. "Sophie's" winning featured 19 Bests of Breed, 3 Group Firsts, and 11 other Group placements. She is the first bitch to win BOB at the ESSC of Michigan Specialty since the club's start in 1934, winning over 22 champions. Bred but once, she is dam of two Best in Show winners.

```
                    Am. & Can. Ch. Salilyn's Citation II
              Ch. Inchidony Prince Charming
                    Ch. Salilyn's Cinderella II
         Ch. Salilyn's Aristocrat
                    Salilyn's Royal Consort
              Ch. Salilyn's Lilly of the Valley
                    Salilyn's Glenda

    CH. SALILYN'S COLONEL'S OVERLORD

                    Ch. Salilyn's Cocktail Time
              Salilyn's Good Fortune
                    Ch. Salilyn's Good Omen
         Ch. Salilyn's Radiance
                    Ch. Salilyn's MacDuff
              Ch. Randalane's Bright Chips
                    Ch. Ascot's Libby
```

Ch. Salilyn's Tennessee Squire, a son of Ch. Salilyn Colonel's Overlord ex Ch. Salilyn's Something Special. Despite his untimely death in September of 1972 (at three years of age), Squire was 4th ranking Springer for that year. His totals included 5 Bests in Show, 26 Group Firsts, and wins of the Keystone and Michigan Specialties. Bred by Mrs. Julia Gasow, he was owned by Mrs. R. V. Clark, Jr. of Middleburg, Va., and handled by Bobby Barlow.

                    Ch. King Peter of Salilyn
    Am. & Can. Ch. Royal Squire of Rexford
                    Ch. Jill of Rexford
    Ch. Geiger's Winaway Duke, U.D.
                    Ch. Melilotus Little Acorn
          Raggedy Ann
          Lee's Bit of Honey
CH. GEIGER'S CHIEF GERONIMO, C.D. - W.D.
                    Ch. Roger of Hunters Hill
    Am. & Can. Ch. Melilotus Argonaut
                    Ch. Tranquillity of Melilotus
    Ch. Schwedekrest Lady Pamela
                    Ch. Melilotus Little Acorn
          Ch. Schwedekrest Forever Genie
          Sonic Genie of Schwedekrest

Firebrand of Sandblown Acre, C.D.X.
Salutation of Salilyn
Am. & Can. Ch. Frejax Royal Salute
Ch. Duchess of Rexford
Ch. Melilotus Royal Oak
Lady Lou of Melilotus
Hunter's Eden Bit O'Blarney
Lady Melissa III
Eng. Am. Can. Ch. Showman of Shotton
Ch. Rufton Pattern
Ch. Gay Skipper
Tranquillity of Well Sweep
Ch. Melilotus Royal Oak
Lady Lou of Melilotus
Ch. Maquam's Ace
Sonic Genie of Coryell

              Am. & Can. Ch. Royal Squire of Rexford
    Ch. Geiger's Winaway Duke, U.D.
              Raggedy Ann
    Ch. Geiger's Chief Geronimo, C.D.
              Am. & Can. Ch. Melilotus Argonaut
    Ch. Schwedekrest Lady Pamela
              Ch. Schwedekrest Forever Genie
AM. & CAN. CH. MAGILL'S PATRICK, C.D. - W.D.X.

              Ch. Melilotus Royal Oak
    Ch. Melilotus Little Acorn
              Lady Lou of Melilotus
    Cindy's Delight
              Tequila Diego
    Diamonds Duchess Delight
              Lady Queen of Diamonds

Ch. King Peter of Salilyn
Ch. Jill of Rexford
Ch. Melilotus Little Acorn
Lee's Bit of Honey
Ch. Roger of Hunters Hill
Ch. Tranquillity of Melilotus
Ch. Melilotus Little Acorn
Sonic Genie of Schwedekrest
Am. & Can. Ch. Frejax Royal Salute
Ch. Tranquillity of Melilotus
Ch. Amos of Melilotus
Ch. Enchantress of Cauliers
Ch. Prince Charlie of Melilotus
Ch. Chula Diega
Jack of Diamonds II
Tippy II

              Ch. Inchidony Prince Charming
    Ch. Salilyn's Aristocrat
              Ch. Salilyn's Lily of the Valley
    Welcome Great Day
              Am. & Can. Ch. Gay Beauties Academy Award
    Ch. Salilyn's Bristol Cream, C.D.X.
              Ch. Salilyn's Good Omen
CH. WELCOME HAPPY TALK

              Ch. Geiger's Winaway Duke, U.D.
    Ch. Geiger's Chief Geronimo, C.D.
              Ch. Schwedekrest Lady Pamela
    Am. & Can. Ch. Flo-Bob's Me Too
              Ch. Jo-Al's White Smoke
    Ch. Belle of Schoodic
              Ch. Wilmar's Show Girl

Ch. Salilyn's Citation II
Ch. Salilyn's Cinderella II
Salilyn's Royal Consort
Salilyn's Glenda
Ch. King Peter of Salilyn
Am. & Can. Ch. Walpride Gay Beauty
Ch. Cartref Bob Bobbin
Salilyn's Surprise
Am. & Can. Ch. Royal Squire of Rexford
Raggedy Ann
Ch. Melilotus Little Acorn
Ch. Schwedekrest Forever Genie
Ch. Runor's Deacon
Jo-Al's Freckles
Ch. Eldgyth Editor
Belfield Evening Star

Am. & Can. Ch. Geiger's Chief Geronimo, C.D., W.D., 1/w, whelped 1959, a top winning dog and important producer on the West Coast. Bred and owned by Tillie Geiger, of North Bend, Washington. Line-bred to Royal Oak on both sides, Geronimo sired 11 champions that are in turn producing many champions. He and his sire, Ch. Geiger's Winaway Duke, U.D. were excellent hunters.

Geronimo's great son, Am. & Can. Ch. Magill's Patrick, C.D., C.D.X., 1/w, whelped 1965, winner of the Sporting Group at Westminster in 1969 under judge Fred Hunt. "Pat's" winning included 4 Bests in Show, 46 Groups, 6 Specialties including Best in Show at the National Specialty and 88 Bests of Breed. Bred and owned by Wayne D. Magill of Renton, Wash. and handled by Eldon McCormack.

Two outstanding Geronimo offspring pictured winning top honors at the 1965 National Specialty held in California. Am. Can. & Mex. Ch. Muller's Blazing Kane (at right) was Best of Breed and Am. & Can. Ch. Flo-Bob's Me Too was Best of Opposite Sex. The two are littermates, whelped 1961 out of Ch. Belle of Schoodle—and this win marked the only time that a litter brother and sister have swept the National. Blazing Kane ("Sam") was a Best in Show winner and Springer of the Year for 1965. The sire of many champions, he is owned by Hazel Westlund, Mountlake Terrace, Washington. Me Too, beautifully presented and handled by her owner Mary Jo Hosteny of Lafayette, California, is dam of distinguished progeny that includes Ch. Welcome Happy Talk, pictured on the facing page.

```
                    Ch. Geiger's Winaway Duke, U.D.
          Am. & Can. Ch. Geiger's Chief Geronimo, C.D.
               Ch. Schwedekrest Lady Pamela
   Am. Can. & Mex. Ch. Muller's Blazing Kane
               Ch. Jo-Al's White Smoke
         Ch. Belle of Schoodic
               Ch. Wilmar's Show Girl

AM., CAN. & MEX. CH. QUIET HILLS SAM'S SON

                    Can. Ch. Toprock Tarquin
         Am. & Can. Ch. Quiet Hills Top Mark
               Ch. Fancy Markette of Liz-Pa Du
   Quiet Hills Bright Side
               Gentleman Dutch
         Dutch's Confetti of Liz-Pa-Du
               Ch. Barrowdale Confetti
```

Ch. Welcome Happy Talk, 1/w, whelped 1968. A son of Ch. Flo-Bob's Me Too, Happy Talk was bred by Mary Jo Hosteny, and is owned by Linda Eckblad. His win of many Groups, and of such Specialties as the Eastern and Potomac Valley, has kept Happy Talk well in the Top Ten of the breed in the early 1970s. Pedigree on Page 216.

Blazing Kane's great w...- ning son, Am. Can. & Mex. Ch. Quiet Hill's Sam's Son, 1/w, whelped 1964, bred, owned and handled by Paul E. Booher of Reno, Nevada. His proud record includes 4 all-breed Bests in Show and 32 Groups.

Ch. Canarch Yankee Patriot, C.D., b/w, owned by Mrs. Robert L. Streng of Farmington, Mich. "Duffy" was guided to his Obedience degree by his owner, and handled to his place with the Top Ten conformation Springers of 1969 (by virtue of strong Specialty and Group wins) by Mike Atkins.

```
                        Ch. Salilyn's Sensation, C.D.
             Am. & Can. Ch. Salilyn's Citation II
                        Salilyn's Princess Meg
          Ch. Inchidony Prince Charming
                        Ch. King Peter of Salilyn
             Ch. Salilyn's Cinderella II
                        Am. & Can. Ch. Walpride Gay Beauty

CH. CANARCH YANKEE PATRIOT, C.D.

                        Ch. Kaintuck Marc Anthony
             Ch. Syringa Disc Jockey
                        Ch. Syringa Sue
          Ch. Canarch Sunnyside, C.D.
                        Ch. Rostherne Hunter
             Melilotus Hufty Tufty
                        Melilotus Princess Dona
```

Ch. Canarch Inchidony Sparkler, b/w, whelped July 4, 1966, bred and owned by Charles Hendee. Pictured winning the Group from the classes at Macomb County show in 1968. Sparkler is a litter brother of Ch. Canarch Yankee Patriot, C.D.

Ch. Benmor's Felicity, one of three champions from the first litter—by Ch. Salilyn's Citation II ex Loujon Princess Meg—bred by the Benmor Kennels of Ed and Joan Morean of Huntsville, Alabama. One of the three, Ch. Benmor's Court Jester, finished in the Top Ten of 1969.

Top, facing page:

Ch. Ascot's Ajax, one of the more famous of the many winning Springers that have come from Leonard Greenwald's Ascot Kennels in South Glastonbury, Connecticut, pictured in his win of the Keystone English Springer Spaniel Club Specialty at Trenton in 1958. A later shining light, the beautiful liver bitch Ch. Ascot's Scarlet O., was Best of Breed at the American Spaniel Club Specialty in 1961.

```
              Kelgate's Hot Toddy             Cartref Count Down
     Ch. Mister Tamridge of Stage Run         Ch. Kelgate's Downy Delight
              Stage Run Mischievous           Ascot's Maverick
Ch. Stage Run Native Son                      Tamridge Nomad
              Ch. Ascot's Emperor             Am. & Can. Ch. Walpride's Flaming Rocket
     Stage Run Miss Miniver, C.D.             Ch. Ascot's Scarlet O
              Stage Run Mischievous           Ascot's Maverick
                                              Tamridge Nomad
CH. TAMRIDGE HOMESTRETCH                       Am. & Can. Ch. Walpride's Flaming Rocket
              Ch. Ascot's Emperor             Ch. Ascot's Scarlet O
     Ch. Ascot's Pimpernel                    Ascot's Maverick
              Ch. Ascot's Scarlet O           Ch. Sunhi's Doody
Tamridge Dubonnet                             Kelgate's Hot Toddy
              Ch. Mister Tamridge of Stage Run Stage Run Mischievous
     Ch. Tamridge Junior Miss, C.D.           Ch. Runor's Trademark
              Tamridge High Button Shoes      Sandolyn's Fantasia
```

Below, facing page:

Ch. Tamridge Homestretch, 1/w, whelped 1966, line-bred to Flaming Rocket through Ascot bloodlines, is pictured here in his win of the Keystone English Springer Spaniel Club Specialty at Trenton in 1970. A frequent Group ribbon winner, Homestretch was bred and is owned by Barbara S. Parker, Tamridge Kennels, Monson, Mass.

```
                    Ch. King William of Salilyn
              Ch. Salilyn's MacDuff
                 Shercliff's Lady Debbie
        Ch. Salilyn's Cocktail Time
                    Ch. King Peter of Salilyn
              Ch. Salilyn's Concerto
                 Ch. Ascot's Estralita
  CH. LOUJON COURVOISIER
                    Ch. Wakefield's Black Knight
              Ch. Loujon Beau of Drewry Lane, C.D.
                 Ch. Cartref Tick Tock of Loujon
        Loujon Lady Bountiful
                    Ch. King William of Salilyn
              Loujon Louise of Crooked Pine, C.D.
                 Loujon's Lightning's Show Girl
```

```
              Ch. Salilyn's Citation II        Ch. Salilyn's Sensation
        Ch. Inchidony Prince Charming          Salilyn's Princess Meg
              Ch. Salilyn's Cinderella II      Ch. King Peter of Salilyn
  Ch. Charlyle's Fair Warning                  Am. & Can. Ch. Walpride's Gay Beauty
              Ch. Banneret's Regal Brigadier   Ch. Ebony of Hillcrest
        Charlyle's Nanette                     Banneret's Gay Festival
              Charlyle's Happy Choice          Salilyn's Young Lochinvar
                                               Ch. Charlyle's Royal Heiress
  CH. DOT'S IT OF MAR-LEN                      Ch. Kaintuck Beau Brummel
              Ch. Kaintuck Christmas Carol     Ch. Cartref Spring Chime
        Ch. Vicar of Wakefield                 Ch. Melilotus Royal Oak
              Ch. Wakefield's Fanny            Judy of Gwynedd
  Ch. Sea Witch                                Ch. Kaintuck Marc Anthony
              Ch. Syringa Disc Jockey          Ch. Syringa Sue
        Ch. Fortune's Dorsue Diana of Day      Ch. Kaintuck Christmas Carol
              Ch. Fortune's Lucky Penny        Ch. Syringa Sue
```

```
                    Ch. Elk Groves Knight Errant
              Ch. Elk Groves Firebrand II
                 Neely's Cinderella
        Ch. Pommie's Black Ramrod
                    Ch. Elk Groves Firebrand Magic
              Elk Groves Royal Holly
                 Favorite II of Caulier's
  CH. RICHMOND'S HUSTLER
                    Ch. Kaintuck Christmas Carol
              Ch. Wakefield's Black Knight
                 Ch. Wakefield's Fanny
        Ch. Richmond's Donna Dee
                    Ch. Crooked Pines Burgoo Boy
              Ch. Loujon Delight
                 Ch. Greeno's Lightning
```

Ch. Loujon Courvoisier (1/w, wh. 1966), whose impressive winning included Best of Breed at the American Spaniel Club Specialty in 1968. "Brandy", bred and owned by Loujon Kennels, goes back to Wakefield Black Knight and Salilyn's Macduff. Handled by Karen Crisanti.

Ch. Richmond's Hustler, 1/w, bred and owned by Jim and Rosemary Wilschke of Clarendon Hills, Illinois. The Hustler has many fine wins including Best of Breed at the 1970 Westminster show. Handled by Jack Funk.

Ch. Anglodale's Mocha Bandit, 1/w, whelped January 1964, highly regarded as a winner and producer on the West Coast. Owned by Alta V. Pleasant of Highland, Calif.

Ch. Whitney's Philosopher, Mocha Bandit's spectacular b/w son, also owned by Alta Pleasant. "Phil" made his start with win of the Futurity at the 1969 National Specialty, and has come on to place in the top echelons of the breed with strong Group and Specialty wins.

```
                Firebrand of Sandblown Acre, C.D.X.   Traveler of Sandblown Acre
      Ch. King William of Salilyn                     Dawn's Elf of Sandblown Acre
          Salutation of Salilyn                       Am. & Can. Ch. Frejax Royal Salute
  Ch. Loresta's Gay Masquerader                       Nancy of Salilyn
          Ch. Briarcliffe Riptide                     Am. & Can. Ch. Frejax Royal Salute
      Ch. Gay Princess Cocoa                          Briarcliffe Bolero
          Ruleon's First Lady                         Am. & Can. Ch. Melilotus Argonaut
CH. ANGLODALE'S MOCHA BANDIT                          Ch. Willow Farm Catalpa
                                                      Ch. Timpanagos Radar
          Ch. Barblythe Top Tune                      Ch. Barblythe Jennifer
      Ch. Lewis Elms Sunny Skylark                    Am. & Can. Ch. Melilotus Argonaut
          Ch. Gypsy Elf of South Riding               Goldie of Idaho
  Kenlor Mocha Minx                                   Ch. Salilyn's Sensation
          Salilyn's Ovation                           Salilyn's Princess Meg
      Kenlor Celeste                                  Ch. Barblythe Top Tune
          Kenlor Audacious Lady                       Kenlor Karen
```

```
                Ch. King William of Salilyn
          Ch. Loresta's Gay Masquerader
              Ch. Gay Princess Cocoa
      Ch. Anglodale's Mocha Bandit
              Ch. Lewis Elms Sunny Skylark
          Kenlor Mocha Minx
              Kenlor Celeste

    CH. WHITNEY'S PHILOSOPHER

              Ch. Salilyn's Citation II
          Am. & Can. Ch. Hillswick Philosopher
              Ch. Hillswick Echo
      Barbara Baby Bandit
              Ch. Ruleon's Duffson
          Ch. Anglodale Mocha Amulet
              Kenlor Kathy
```

```
              Ch. Kaintuck Prince Hamlet
          Ch. Kaintuck Marc Anthony
              Kaintuck Roxane
      Ch. Syringa Disc Jockey
              Ch. Runor's Deacon
          Ch. Syringa Sue
              Ch. Her Ladyship of Melilotus
    CH. FORTUNE'S DORSUE DIANA OF DAY
              Ch. Cartref Beau Brummel
          Ch. Kaintuck Christmas Carol
              Ch. Cartref Spring Chime
      Ch. Fortune's Lucky Penny
              Ch. Runor's Deacon
          Ch. Syringa Sue
              Ch. Her Ladyship of Melilotus
```

Ch. Fortune's Dorsue Diana of Day, b/w, whelped 1963. This lovely bitch had many good wins during her show career, and has been a valuable producer of champions. Bred by Jeanne Dayton, and owned by Dorothy Fortuna, Huntington, N.Y. (Pedigree, Page 227.)

Ch. Marjon's Sparkling Challenge, an important winner on the West Coast until his unfortunate death at peak of his career. His progeny continue effectively for his owners, Peggy and Vern Johnson, of Orange, California.

Ch. Gay Princess Cocoa, W.D.
(l/w). A Best of Opposite Sex
winner at Specialties in her show-
time, Cocoa was the parent club
"Dam of the Year" for 1961, and
dam of 7 champions. Owned by
Edward and Lillian Stapp, of
Fontana, California. Two of Cocoa's best known winning offspring, also owned by Mr. and
Mrs. Stapp's Loresta Kennels, are
pictured below.

Ch. Loresta's Gay Promenader,
l/w, by Ch. King William of Salilyn ex Ch. Gay Princess Cocoa.
Promenader, BOB winner and
Group contender, is shown finish-
ing his championship with a 5-
point major at Harbor Cities KC
in 1961.

Ch. Loresta's Gay Request, l/w
bitch, by Ch. Salilyn's Macduff ex
Ch. Gay Princess Cocoa, consis-
tent BOB and BOS winner. Shown
scoring Best Opposite at the
Greater California English Springer
Spaniel Club Specialty at Beverly-
Riviera KC, 1964.

Ch. Ramsgate's Scotch Mist, 1/w, whelped 1967. "Scotty's" very impressive winning included Best in Show at the National Specialty, 9 all-breed BIS, and 37 Group Firsts in a period of 16 months. By Ch. Inchidony Prince Charming ex Delledo Merry Mark, C.D., bred and owned by Richard and Janice Mau.

Ch. Waiterock Firebow, bred and owned by Juanita Waite Howard. This lovely bitch was not only a bench champion, but also had many placements in licensed field trials. Pictured here at ten, at which age she achieved the parent club working certificate.—*photo, Jerry Baldwin.*

Am. Can. & Bda. Ch. Oaktree's Lancashire Poacher, b/w, bred and owned by Anne Snelling of Ottawa, Canada. Poacher is the only Canadian bred and owned Springer to win Group and other placements in the United States in recent years. He is handled by William J. Trainor.

Ch. Beaujeu Renown, l/w dog, whelped 1967, Best in Show and frequent Group winner. Owned by Billy D. Evans, Devan Kennels, Plano, Texas. Renown is the sire of Best in Show winner Ch. Devan Fitzpatrick.

Ch. Dot's It of Mar Len, lovely b/w bitch, whelped 1967. After completing her championship with a 5-point BOS win over Specials bitches at the 1969 Eastern Specialty, Dot's It compiled a record that included win of the Group, 7 BOBs and 25 important Eastern BOS wins including 3 Specialties and Westminster. Owned by Mary Ellen Bates and handled by Dorothy Callahan.

Ch. Salilyn's Santa Claus, a beloved house pet of the Ziessow family of Franklin, Michigan. This liver/white dog did not start his show career until he was over five years old, but then amassed a total of 9 Bests in Show, 28 Group Firsts, and many other Group placements. He was No. 2 Springer in the Phillips Ratings for 1965, and No. 6 of all Sporting Dogs.

Ch. Frejax Bit of Old Blighty, C.D.X., l/w, 1959–1970. By Ch. Frejax Royalist ex Ch. Frejax Supreme Challenge, this important producer represented the last of the Frejax line. Bred and owned by Mary Jo Hosteny of Lafayette, California.

Ch. Salilyn's Repeater II, l/w. "Rep", a dearly loved member of the V. L. Atkins "family", Ann Arbor, Michigan. He had several Sporting Group wins through the age of eight years.

```
                    Traveler of Sandblown Acre
             Firebrand of Sandblown Acre, C.D.X.
                    Dawn's Elf of Sandblown Acre
          Ch. King Peter of Salilyn
                    Am. & Can. Ch. Frejax Royal Salute
             Salutation of Salilyn
             Nancy of Salilyn
  CH. SALILYN'S SANTA CLAUS
                    Ch. Ever Rest's Royal Flush
             Ch. Sunhi's Christmas Star
                    Ch. Melilotus Golden Wedding
          Ch. Salilyn's Evening Star
                    Ch. Salilyn's Sensation, C.D.
             Salilyn's Surprise
             Salutation of Salilyn
```

```
                    Firebrand of Sandblown Acre, C.D.X.
             Ch. King Peter of Salilyn
             Salutation of Salilyn
          Ch. Frejax Royalist
                    Ch. Sir Lancelot of Salilyn
             Frejax Lilac Model
                    Ch. Frejax Lilac Time
  CH. FREJAX BIT OF OLD BLIGHTY, C.D.X.
                    Am. & Can. Ch. Frejax Royal Salute
             Ch. Frejax Royal Request
             Frejax Apache Star
          Ch. Frejax Supreme Challenge
                    Am. & Can. Ch. Frejax Royal Salute
             Ch. Frejax Royal Supreme II
             Frejax Judy
```

```
                    Traveler of Sandblown Acre
             Firebrand of Sandblown Acre, C.D.X.
                    Dawn's Elf of Sandblown Acre
          Ch. King Peter of Salilyn
                    Am. & Can. Ch. Frejax Royal Salute
             Salutation of Salilyn
             Nancy of Salilyn
  CH. SALILYN'S REPEATER II
                    Ch. Co-Pilot of Sandblown Acre
             Ch. Sir Lancelot of Salilyn
             Nancy of Salilyn
          Frejax Delightful
                    Am. & Can. Frejax Royal Salute
             Lilac of Happy Days
                    Ch. Runor's Alexis
```

```
            Ch. Chaltha's The Gainer          Ch. Co-Pilot of Sandblown Acre
    Am. & Can. Ch. Walpride Flaming Rocket    Ch. Chaltha's Hope
        Walpride Sensation                    Dormond Dark Danger
Ch. Ascot's Emperor Jones                     Dormond Gypsy
        Ascot's Maverick                      Am. & Can. Ch. Walpride Flaming Rocket
    Ch. Ascot's Scarlet O                     Ascot's Diamond Lil
        Ch. Sunhi's Doody                     Ch. Sunhi's Christmas Star
CH. BERYLTOWN BOLD CRUSADER                   Sunhi's Duchess

            Ch. Chaltha's The Gainer          Ch. Co-Pilot of Sandblown Acre
    Am. & Can. Ch. Walpride Flaming Rocket    Ch. Chaltha's Hope
        Walpride Sensation                    Dormond Dark Danger
Ch. Beryltown Lively Rocket                   Dormond Gypsy
        Ch. Prince Charlie of Melilotus       Am. & Can. Ch. Frejax Royal Salute
    Ch. Cartref Donla's Arpege, C.D.          Ch. Tranquillity of Melilotus
        Ch. Cartref Tali Hi                   Ch. Cartref Wizard
                                              Ch. Cartref Chimneysweep
```

```
                Ch. King William of Salilyn
            Ch. Salilyn's Macduff
                Shercliffe's Lady Debbie
        Ch. Salilyn's Cocktail Time
                Ch. King Peter of Salilyn
            Ch. Salilyn's Concerto
                Ch. Ascot's Estralita

CH. SALILYN'S SIR MARIC SUPREME, C.D.

                Ch. King Peter of Salilyn
            Ch. Salilyn's Repeater II
                Frejax Delightful
        Salilyn's Repetition
                Ch. Cartref Bob Bobbin
            Ch. Salilyn's Good Omen
                Salilyn's Surprise
```

```
            Ch. Salilyn's Sensation, C.D.     Am. & Can. Ch. Frejax Royal Request
    Am. & Can. Ch. Salilyn's Citation II      Queen Victoria of Salilyn
        Salilyn's Princess Meg                Ch. King Peter of Salilyn
Ch. Inchidony Prince Charming                 Ch. Salilyn's Animation II
        Ch. King Peter of Salilyn             Firebrand of Sandblown Acre, C.D.X.
    Ch. Salilyn's Cinderella II               Salutation of Salilyn
        Am. & Can. Ch. Walpride Gay Beauty    Ch. Chalta's The Gainer
AM. & CAN. CH. PEMBROKE INCHIDONY SCOT, C.D.  Walpride Sensation

        Ch. King Peter of Salilyn             Firebrand of Sandblown Acre, C.D.X.
    Ch. Salilyn's Santa Claus                 Salutation of Salilyn
        Ch. Salilyn's Evening Star            Ch. Sunhi's Christmas Star
Ch. Phyliss Duchess of Pembroke, C.D.         Salilyn's Surprise
        Ch. Salilyn's Sensation, C.D.         Am. & Can. Ch. Frejax Royal Request
    Grande Pointe's First Lady                Queen Victoria of Salilyn
        Ch. Gay Beauties Princess Pat, C.D.   Ch. King Peter of Salilyn
                                              Am. & Can. Ch. Walpride Gay Beauty
```

Ch. Salilyn's Sir Maric Supreme, C.D., l/w, whelped 1965, repeat Best in Show winner. Owned by Madeline Jente, St. Louis, Missouri. Madeline and husband Dick have sure done well by this, their first show Springer.

Ch. Pembroke Inchidony Scot, C.D., a Prince Charming son ex Ch. Phyliss Duchess of Pembroke, C.D. Whelped in 1968, Scot was one of the leading winners of the early '70s with a score of 9 Bests in Show, 37 Group Firsts and a Specialty all within 16 months. Owned by Alice Berd (breeder) and Donald Robb, and handled by Robert Schmitz.

Ch. Loresta's Storm King, parent club "Dog of the Year" for 1972. Storm King was winner of the GCESSA Specialty in both '72 and '73. By Aristocrat ex Ch. Loresto's Lady Cynthia, he was bred and is owned by Edward M. and Lillian R. Stapp of Fontana, California, and handled by Ray McGinnis.

Ch. El Taro's Scotch Flag, the top winning English Springer Spaniel of 1973. In just over half the year, his wins included 36 out of 40 Bests of Breed, a Best in Show, 10 Groups and 3 Specialty BOBs. Whelped January 1969, he is by Ch. Salilyn's Signature ex Beryltown Gingersnap of Taro, C.D. Bred by Elva M. Taisey, and owned by Earl Taisey of Poolesville, Maryland, and handled by George Alston.

Ch. Salilyn's Vanguard, whelped November 1971, by Aristocrat ex Ch. Salilyn's Tiffany. At less than two years, "Van" had already won 4 Sporting Groups. Bred and owned by Julia Gasow and Barbara Jane Gates.

Ch. Salilyn's Classic, whelped June 1971, by Ch. Salilyn's Encore ex Salilyn's Arista. At just past two, "Chip" stood as winner of an all-breed Best in Show and 4 Group Firsts, including one from puppy class. Pictured going Best of Breed at the English Springer Spaniel Field Trial Association National Specialty in August 1973, under judge Mrs. James E. Clark. Bred and owned by Julia Gasow and Barbara Gates, and handled by Miss Gates.

Ch. Kaintuck Pixie, one of the few bitches that has been able to win Best of Breed over male champions. Bred by the late Stuart Johnson, this liver/white is owned by Anne Pope Anders of Boston.

Ch. Kaintuck Heir Apparent, whelped 1968, Best of Breed from the classes at the 1971 American Spaniel Club Specialty under all-breeds judge, Mrs. Winifred Heckmann. Heir Apparent was bred by Patricia Schoonmaker, and is co-owned by Mrs. W. J. S. Borie and D. Lawrence Carswell (his handler).

17
The Springer
in Obedience

THE SPRINGER'S high intelligence and merry temperament make him a top-working Obedience dog. Obedience training offers many advantages, not the least of which is making your dog a more enjoyable, well-behaved companion. It also holds tremendous appeal and fascination in that, if properly trained, you can enter him in the exciting competition of Obedience trials.

Before starting on an Obedience program, bear in mind that the Springer Spaniel has an essentially soft temperament and, as a rule, will not take severe corrections. Avoid punishment—be lavish with praise. The techniques effective in training larger Working breeds are not applicable to Springer Spaniels.

Enroll in an Obedience training club or school, preferably one for Springers only. Today there is scarcely an area that does not have some group with the common objective of training dogs to be better behaved companions, or of working toward the coveted AKC Obedience degrees—C.D. (Companion Dog); C.D.X. (Companion Dog Excellent); U.D. (Utility Dog), and U.D.T. (Utility Dog Tracker).

Of obvious assistance in the training of your dogs is a good book on the subject, and there are several that we recommend. One of the best is "Training You to Train Your Dog" by Blanche Saunders, founder of Obedience training as we know it in America today. An excellent and more recent work is "The Pearsall Guide to Successful Dog

Training" by Margaret E. Pearsall. The Pearsall methods are particularly interesting in that they are based on keeping the dog's "point of view" in mind—awareness of the dog's physical capabilities and limitations, and of what dog psychology has taught us of his behavior patterns. (Both of these books are available from Howell Book House, Inc., 730 Fifth Avenue, New York, N.Y. 10019.) Also recommended are "Training Your Spaniel" by Clarence Pfaffenberger and "Trials Without Tribulations" by Margo Ande.

If it is your intention to enter your Springer in Obedience trials, send for the booklet "Obedience Regulations", which will explain the necessary details and requirements as set down by the American Kennel Club. A free copy may be obtained by writing to The American Kennel Club, 51 Madison Avenue, New York, N.Y. 10010

Some knowledgeable people insist that Obedience training will not interfere with showing your Springer in conformation. Rather, if properly trained, the dog will handle *more* confidently in a show ring with other dogs. However, it is vital that prime consideration be given to temperament. Too heavy a training hand will subdue the spirit so essential in a winning show dog.

Even the smartest, best performing Springer will leave a bad impression if he is dirty and untrimmed. Too often we hear, "Oh, he is only entered in Obedience." Never forget that there are often as many people watching the Obedience ring at a show as the conformation ring. The Springer Spaniel *as a breed* is being judged by the public in both rings, and should be well represented.

Sally of Duckenfield, U.D.T.
(Ch. Frejax Top Hole of Blighty ex Duckenfield Princess)
1/w—whelped, November 1, 1940

Sally made history as the first U.D.T. Springer Spaniel in the United States. In scoring her C.D., C.D.X., U.D. and Tracking degrees all within a span from March 1 to September 26, 1942 she set a record that not only stands for Springers, but may well stand for all breeds. Sally also won water retrieving competitions. Bred by Lillian and Albert Robinson, and owned by Charles A. Frank of Detroit.

Henry of Navarre, C.D., C.D.X.
(whelped May, 1940)

Shown here clearing a height of 42 inches, which he did with ease, Henry was a top Obedience star in an era when that competition was dominated by the Working breeds. A grandson of Ch. Dunoon Donald Dhu, he was obviously not a conformation specimen, but more than proved himself in intelligence and Obedience skills. Most important of all, he was the beginning interest in English Springers for his owners, Becher and Dorothy Hungerford, whose success with Ch. Inchidony Prince Charming is told on Page 167.

"Obedience Springer of The Year"

Each year the English Springer Spaniel Field Trial Association, parent club of the breed, awards a Certificate of Merit to the "Obedience Springer of The Year", won by the dog with the highest total score for the preceding year.

If one studies the breeding of these winners it is evident that they are from widely different areas and completely different breeding. Unlike the situation in conformation, the Obedience Springer competition is not dominated by a few big-name kennels. It would seem that no line has a monopoly on Springer intelligence.

Here are the dogs honored as "Springer of The Year" since inauguration of the award in 1959:

1959:   Fleishman's Spectacular, U.D.
        owned by (Mr. and Mrs. A. Fleishman, Spokane, Wash.)
1960:   Pussy Willow Sir Skeeter
        owned by (R. G. Leonard, Adrian, Mich.)
1961:   Bal Lakes Lady Patricia, U.D.
        Edson Bahr, Edmonds, Wash.)
1962:   Bal Lakes Lady Patricia, U.D.
1963:   Bal Lakes Lady Patricia, U.D.
1964:   Bal Lakes Lady Patricia, U.D.
1965:   Tie: Loujon Deuce of Charlemar, C.D.X., W.D.
            (Kay Crisanti, New Richmond, Ohio)
        and   La Belle Don Mitzi
            (Judy Lundbeck, Fargo, N.D.)
1966:   Tie: Ch. Walpride Karrie of Charlemar, C.D.X., W.D.
            (Kay Crisanti, New Richmond, Ohio)
        and   Loujon Deuce of Charlemar, C.D.X., W.D.
1967:   La Belle Don Mitzi, C.D.X.
1968:   La Belle Don Mitzi, U.D.
1969:   Tigaria Pamper, U.D.
        (Ruth Wallace, Riverdale, Ill.)
1970:   Loujon Lord Kelvin, U.D.
        (Theresa Luley, Indianapolis, Ind.)
1971:   Ch. New Dawn of Marjon, U.D.
        (C. Thistel, Annapolis, Md.)
        Note: New Dawn won her C.D., C.D.X. and U.D. in one year.
1972:   Nancy's Fancy Lady, U.D.
        (Laurence J. Libeu, Garden Grove, Calif.)

Showing the English Springer Spaniel: Dorothy Callahan, who
together with her husband, Clint, make up one of the very many
husband-and-wife teams of professional handlers, here presents Ch.
Anastasia of Berclee under the judging of the author at the 1967
Eastern Specialty. Anastasia, owned by Bernice Roe of Spencerville,
Maryland, was Best of Opposite Sex.

18
Showing Your Springer

ALTHOUGH the main purpose of dog shows is to promote the breeding of purebred dogs, the showing of dogs has become a sport of major importance. It offers what is for many the opportunity of achievement as meaningful as the Olympics, and competition as exciting as the World Series.

Fundamentally, when you pay an entry fee at a dog show, you pay for the judge's opinion of your dog. His decision will be based upon how closely your dog conforms to the official standard of the breed, in comparison to the others in his ring. The American Kennel Club suggests a time allowance of less than three minutes for the judging of each dog, so it is essential that you have your entry looking his best and showing to advantage whenever the judge's glance happens to come his way.

This calls for homework. Ring manners can be taught fairly easily. For instance, any dog can learn to walk on a leash—but the important thing is how he does it. A top show dog loves the ring and therefore moves with style and spirit. To accomplish this end result you must have patience, and be willing to take things slowly, never making a "duty" of his lessons. The secret of making a showman is to keep the illusion, forever, that this is a "fun-game".

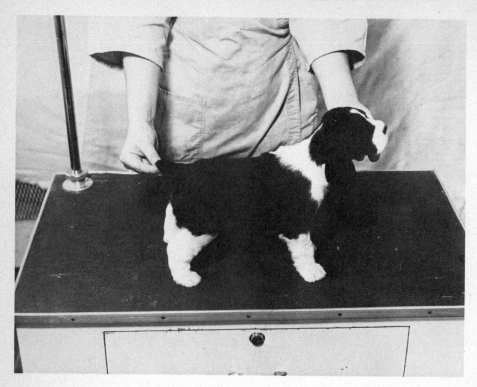

Training the Puppy for Show

A puppy's training can begin as soon as he is able to walk steadily. Stand him on a table and, while you hold his head up with your left hand, use your right hand to *very gently and slowly* distribute his weight evenly on all four legs. In a surprisingly short time, he will learn to hold this pose alone with merely a touch of your finger under his chin and his tail.

By the time he is seven weeks old, your puppy should be acquainted with a show lead. Use a soft 1/4-inch Resco variety. Children do well leash-breaking puppies. However, they must be emphatically cautioned never to pull or jerk the leash. The puppy must enjoy what he is doing and as soon as he begins to tire, the lesson must end.

I cannot emphasize too strongly the benefits of entering your dog in licensed matches and conformation classes, and of accustoming him to riding with you in the car, and to crowds and noises of all kinds. Last, but far from least, it is important to introduce him to a dog crate, for remember, at dog shows he must live in one.

TRIMMING THE SPRINGER
FOR SHOW

Okay, now your dog has learned to stand willingly for inspection, knows how to move gaily on a lead, and is accustomed to the general confusion he will face at a dog show. *You* must now learn how to help him win. It is up to you to present him in such a way that he will stand out—that he, above the other dogs, will attract the judge's attention in that vital moment when the dogs are first moved around the ring together. To do this, you must learn the art of trimming and grooming a Springer for show.

At this point, I suggest you turn to the chapter of this book in which the official breed standard is presented (Page 271). Only when you have a picture of the "ideal" Springer firmly in your mind can you learn how to trim one. The standard itself is your trimming chart. Follow it explicitly, taking off hair only to sculpture your Springer to its image.

I call your attention to one paragraph in particular:

> "*To be penalized:* Rough curly coat. Overtrimming, especially of body coat. Any chopped, barbered, or artificial effect. Excessive feathering that destroys the clean outline desirable in a sporting dog."

Time Schedule for Show Trimming

If a dog is completely untrimmed, the work should be done in three stages, starting two full weeks before the show.

Otherwise, trim your Springer one week before a show. The *day* before the show give him a general "touch-up", but do not use a clippers. The hair on his head and clippered areas will have grown out sufficiently to give him a natural look and to enable you to even out any nicks or lines you may have left.

Electric Clippers

(*Note: The figures in parentheses in the following instructions indicate the areas identified by these figures in the drawing on photo diagram on the facing page.*)

Assuming your dog has had a bath, is thoroughly combed and free of all tangles and mats, begin the clipper work.

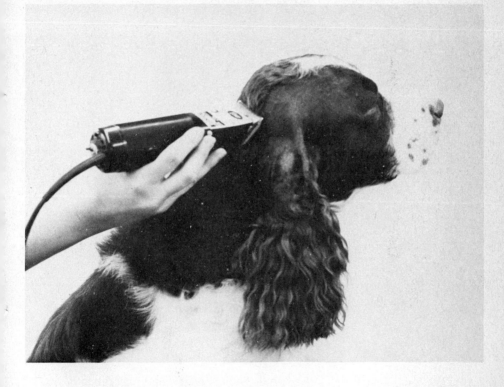

Use a Number 10 blade. Start with the ears. From a line even with the eye (1) move the clippers upward against the grain of the hair.

Still working against the grain, take the clippers over the occipital bone (2), down over the stop (3), and into the groove between the eyes.

The head should be cleaned with the clippers around and beneath the eyes to accentuate chiseling, over the flues and lips, taking off the whiskers, around the corners of the mouth for neatness, and under the ears to make them hang close to the cheeks.

Hold the dog's head in your hand and look at him from the front. Have you made your trimming line the same on both ears? Make sure

they balance. Then blend your starting line on each ear by taking the clippers downward over it, *with* the grain of the hair, for about 1/2 inch. This will lower the placement of the ears on the head.

Blend your starting line on the head by going down over it from the occipital bone, *with* the grain, on the top of the neck to point (5).

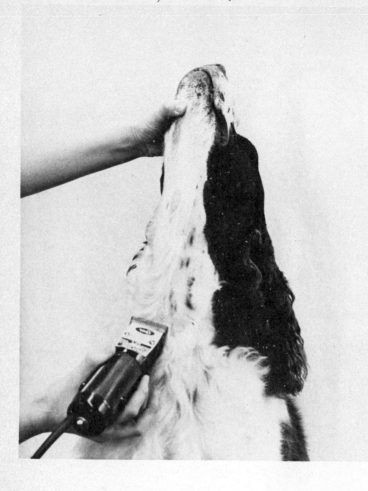

Next, trim upward, against the grain, from about three inches above the breast bone (4) on up under the neck and chin.

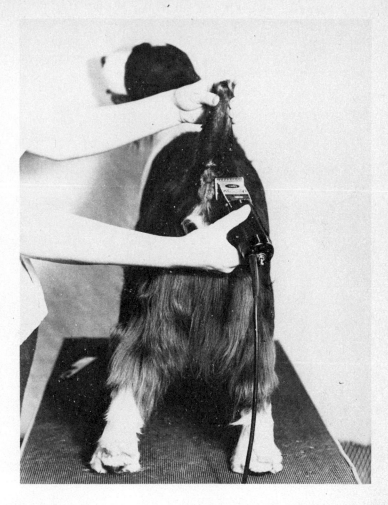

The clippers may also be used under the tail *with* the grain of the hair.

NEVER, BUT NEVER, TOUCH THE CLIPPERS TO THE BODY OF THE DOG.

Thinning Shears

Use of this tool requires practice for perfection. A medium weight, single-blade thinning shears gives best results and should be handled as if you were a barber trimming the back of a man's head.

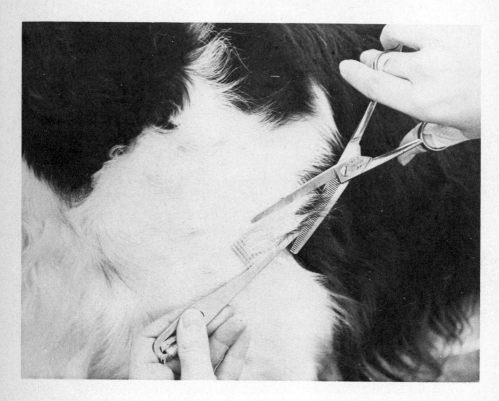

Hold a "medium" tooth steel comb in your left hand and lift up the hair. As you move the comb upward against the grain, cut the ends of the hair above the comb. Comb the hair back down after each cutting. Repeat the procedure until the hair is the desired length.

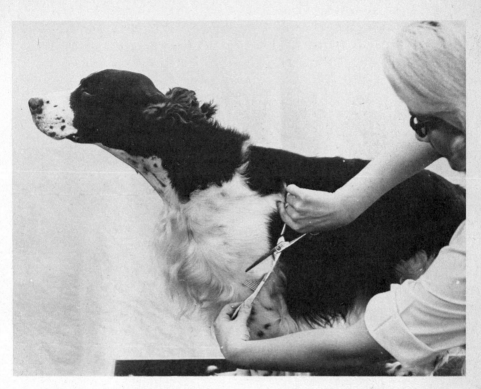

Begin body thinning at the elbow, working upward over the shoulder toward the neck, where you must blend out the line left by the clippers.

The clipper line at the occipital bone must now be carefully blended into the neck. Beware of the white hair—it has a tricky way of showing scissor marks! Leave the hair longer as you go down, on top of the neck, to softly cover the shoulder blades. There should be no break to show where the neck ends, but rather, the neck should be trimmed to gradually blend into the shoulders.

"The back to be straight and strong, with no tendency to dip or roach" says the standard. Trim accordingly. To help overcome a possible "dip", leave all the hair *on* in that particular spot, thinning in front of it and behind it.

The unpleasing "roached" back can be greatly improved by taking off as much hair as possible over the rump. Hair usually grows thicker in this area and if the top line is *good,* we merely thin it lightly to give a smooth appearance. Thin and blend over and around the tail, and thin excess feathering beneath the tail.

Stand back and look at your work frequently if possible, trim in front of a mirror.

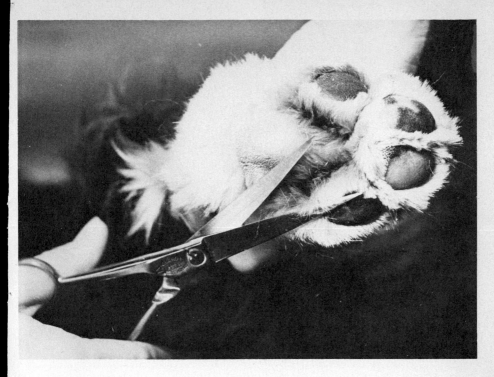

Trimming Feet

A regular straight scissors is used on the feet. Pick up each foot and take off the hair underneath.

Cut around the foot to make it look as round and compact and neat as you can.

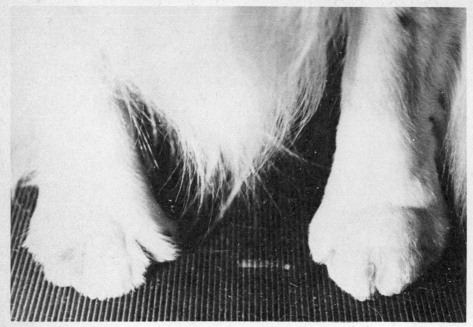

The "before-and-after" of trimming the feet of the English Springer. At left, an
untrimmed foot; at right, a trimmed one.

Use thinning shears to remove excess hair on hocks, but leave enough
hair to soften and round the top of the hock.

The nails should be trimmed with a nail clipper or filed.

The "Glamour" Touch—
Final Bath

Your dog must be bathed the night before the show, preferably late,
after his last outing, and the procedure is equally as important as
trimming.

Use a good name brand shampoo recommended for dry hair—we
use Halo. Never use cake soap. Suds twice and rinse thoroughly, paying
special attention to removing all traces of soap under elbows and ears.

After rinsing, squeeze out as much water as possible from the dog,
in the tub. Put two full tablespoons of straight glycerin into an average
size feeding pan of warm water. Mix well and carefully "pat" this down
the dog's back and sides. Then dip the ears in the remainder and pat

them over the head and neck. Work this into the coat with your hands. Do not rinse off.

Use towels for drying—not an electric dryer. Comb completely while still damp, and when the hair on the back is perfectly in place, "blanket" the dog tightly and put him in a dog crate on *white paper* for the night. This is unprinted newspaper, purchased at any newspaper office, and well worth its price, as ink rubs off of regular newspaper stock to dull that pure white you must have to give your Springer flash.

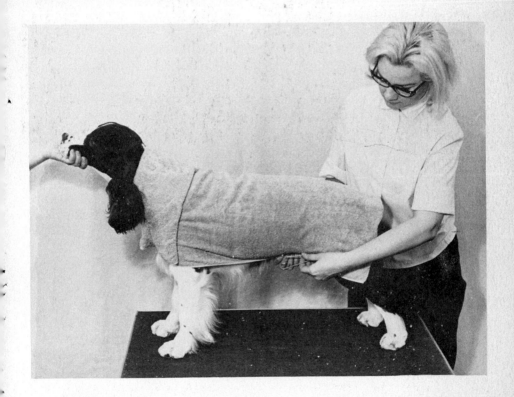

How To Blanket Your Dog

For blanketing our dog, we will need a bath towel and three blanket pins. The towel, or terry cloth jacket, should be of medium weight and wide enough to go around the dog's body. Some jackets fasten with tapes that cross underneath and tie on top; I do not care for these because they leave a line when the dog is dry.

Blanket pins are to be found at the notions counter in most department stores.

Fold the towel back, collar fashion, and pin under the neck. Carefully smooth hair once more on the back before laying towel down to tail. Pull snugly around rib cage and pin underneath. The last pin is used up under the loin to hold the towel tight over the back.

When the blanket is removed in the morning, your dog will have a smoothness and sparkling sheen that will delight you.

Conditioning Springer Coat

Coat is a mirror of the health and condition *inside* your dog. Good food in adequate quantity is essential for prime condition, which is reflected in blemish-free skin and soft, shining hair—winter and summer.

However, the change of seasons calls for judgment and a little extra coat care. For instance, direct rays of the summer sun can be the ruination of a show coat. Not only will the liver dogs fade when subjected to constant sun, but the blacks under the same conditions will take on a henna hue that is most undesirable. And the body coats of both will become dry and harsh.

If your show dogs are kenneled in unshaded runs, exercise them early in the morning and after sundown.

And I suggest that you keep a small amount of oil on the coat through the entire summer. Johnson's Baby Oil serves well as a base, and with a small amount of Glover's Mange Cure added to it, will do as much good as any "formula" you can find.

Mother Nature gives dogs that live outside in winter a very heavy coat. She does this for their protection against the cold, with no thought in mind of coming dog shows! This is a coat of extremely dense underfur and dry, bristly guard-hair—an unmanageable combination that will take several months to control. Forget showing a dog in March that has lived outside through the winter.

19
The Springer as a Pet

Now perhaps you have no interest in field trials or dog shows, nor the patience to train a dog for Obedience. You might only be looking for a dog to be a member of your family—a pal—one that wants to please you, go wherever you go and do what you want to do. One, too, that will be good with the children and can be easily housebroken. You might also enjoy taking him hunting once or twice a year, though you have no time to actually train him for the field.

Then an English Springer Spaniel fills your bill. He is a natural in the field and can hunt all day with enthusiasm; yet, being of medium size, he is ideal in the home or car, and can easily adjust himself to any mode of living. Many Springers live in apartments, getting their exercise on leash or in the park.

This is a sturdy breed. Usually they are good eaters and can live indoors or out. But to thrive, a Springer must have human companionship. He is a happy fellow with a merry tail, eagerly anticipating your next move so that he can please you. Feed him well, love him, and he will repay you tenfold.

Buying a puppy is a thrilling and exciting experience, but for some it is a frightening responsibility as well. We have compiled some of the questions most frequently asked us by new owners, and perhaps answering them can help smooth the way for others.

But first, some general suggestions. Be prepared when you buy your Springer puppy to devote two or three days to properly orienting him. His habits must be established the first day you bring him home. It is far easier to *train* him than to *untrain* him.

Gentleness and repetition do the trick. No slapping, please. No newspapers. Just one word—"No!"—in a sturdy "I-mean-it" tone of voice.

A crate of suitable size is a wise investment, whether it is the folding wire variety or plywood. Feed and sleep him in it. This comes to be his own secure domain, greatly facilitates housebreaking him, prevents him from chewing or causing damage when left alone, and is the answer to rainy days when he comes in with muddy feet!

Play ball with your puppy from the beginning, coaxing him to bring the object back to you. He will love the "game" and be getting the best kind of exercise, particularly if he lives in an apartment. Moreover, this teaches him to "retrieve". He can soon be taught to "come" when called and, later, to "lie down". It is a pleasure to own a well-mannered house dog.

Don't give him bones. They cause too many kinds of trouble, much beyond their worth. But by all means give the puppy something to chew; any rawhide toys are good, particularly "Chew bars".

Now let us answer some of the questions most often asked by new puppy buyers:

How much do I feed my puppy? How often do I feed him? What do I feed him?

An 8-week old Springer puppy should eat 1 1/2 to 2 lbs. of mixed food a day, divided into three meals, plus 1/2 to 1 can of evaporated milk.

2 parts dry food
1 part meat } Meat and
water weigh
1 part water } the same

Cover the dry food with very hot water and soak 15 minutes. Add meat and mix thoroughly. The consistency of the mixture is important. If too stiff or dry it will stick to the puppy's mouth, but if too sloppy it will have a laxative effect. The mixture should be soft and almost "fluffy".

When the puppy has finished his meal, or most of it, puncture a can of Pet or Carnation milk and pour some, *undiluted,* in the same pan.

Feeding time should be regular—as close as possible to the same time each day.

Between 9 weeks and 3 months, your puppy should consume 2 1/2 lbs. of mixed food a day. Shortly thereafter, 3 lbs. of food a day. As you increase his morning meal he will show less interest in his noon meal, at which time you may divide the full amount into two meals instead of three a day.

Never decrease the amount of food. Growing dogs need food more than adults. Some active young dogs at the ages of between 10 months and two years will eat 4 lbs. of wet food to satisfy their caloric requirement for show condition. Your puppy will love all table scraps and they may be added to his regular diet, particularly bits of fat and gravy. Cooked eggs and cottage cheese are excellent foods for him.

How often should he have a bath?

Whenever you think he needs one. Use a "people's" shampoo, rinse him thoroughly, dry him well and keep him out of drafts.

What about distemper and other vaccines?

Today all veterinarians adminster a very effective modified tissue culture vaccine against *distemper* and *hepatitis*. This has effectively erased fear of exposure at dog shows to these dreaded infections. You are familiar with the serious, and often fatal, symptons of canine distemper. Infectious canine hepatitis is a virus disease equally as serious. This hepatitus virus is specific to dogs, and not related to human hepatitis.

Often veterinarians combine distemper and hepatitis vaccine with a bacterin effective against *leptospirosis,* a disease thought to be transmitted in some instances by rats.

The conscientious administration of the above vaccines has almost entirely eliminated these extremely serious dog diseases.

At our kennel we have abandoned the use of *homologus* serum as a "temporary" immunizer. And we find no indication for measles vaccine. Follow the recommendations of your veterinarian regarding immunization of your puppy.

Puppies, like babies, have a maternal immunity lasting for 6 weeks to sometimes 3 months of age. As a precaution, we give a tissue culture vaccine as early as 6 or 7 weeks and to further the assurance of good immunity, we have a second vaccine given at another 2 or 3 week interval, and a third 2 or 3 weeks later.

Ask your veterinarian to issue a certificate and request him to remind you to return for yearly booster vaccines of distemper, hepatitis and leptospirosis to keep high immunity against those diseases.

Has the puppy been wormed?

Yes, three times. At 5 weeks, 6 weeks, and 7 weeks of age. However, it is advisable to have your veterinarian run a fecal check in about 3 months. All worms (except tapeworms) produce characteristic eggs or ova readily detected under a microscope.

Tapeworm eggs are voided in small segments or packets passed on the outside of the stool. Sometimes the dried tapeworm packets are found on the hair underneath the tail.

Specific vermicides or vermifuges are available for each of the parasites we wish to eliminate. They must be administered with judgment. If used injudiciously they are capable of being toxic, causing dizziness, coma, diarrhea, kidney and liver damage. Use under the supervision of your veterinarian.

Should I take any precaution against heartworm?

Heartworm infestation in dogs is receiving increasing attention. Details concerning the life cycle and *spread* of this parasite are available from veterinarians and veterinary literature.

Heartworm infestation in years past was considered primarily a warm climate or tropical disease, but today, our Northern dogs are being infected with this parasite.

A blood examination by your veterinarian each Spring during the months of March or April is certainly to be recommended. In the Northern states, some areas show a very low incidence of heartworm. For example, possibly 1.5% of the dog population. The disease is endemic in other areas, and infestations of over 25% of the dog population are reported.

Administration of daily preventative medication must be decided between you, as the owner, and your veterinarian. Treatment of infected dogs is possible, and veterinarians approach these cases with care and consideration.

Is it true that Springers have ear problems?

Springers have pendant ears, and consequently less ventilation than in a short-eared or prick-eared dog. The ear canal of your puppy should be whitish-pink, free from debris and wax, and free from odor. The dark wax which sometimes accumulates in puppy ears, can be removed with Q-tips dipped in baby oil. Dogs have long ear canals and the eardrum is situated around the side of the ear canal. Consequently, the applicator can be inserted to its full length without causing injury. This point must be emphasized to mothers who, of course, use extreme care in cleaning their baby's ears. Ear infections are caused by bacteria, by parasites, and by fungus infections. Treatment of these more serious problems must be handled by a veterinarian.

Is it true that Springers shed a great deal?

Shedding is a problem that dog owners of all breeds experience to some degree. Hair growth in animals is not a constant process, but a phasic one. In the first part of the phase, the hair is actively growing. In the second part, the growth stops and the hair goes into a resting stage. The resting hair is sooner or later shed and the follicle is left empty in preparation for the next growth phase.

Typically the dog goes through two growing and resting phases each year. The obvious is the resting phase associated with the spring shedding. Since dogs are now often kept inside most of the year, the cycles become less distinct until the animal sheds all year around.

Illness or stresses such as pregnancy may cause a dog's hair to go into a resting stage and shed. Regrowth will occur when the hair enters the next growth phase if the underlying stress is gone.

Excessive shedding may just be a variation of the normal, but should be checked for possible skin disease. Good health, a well-balanced diet and brushing all help.

We could not housebreak our last puppy because of constant diarrhea. Have you any suggestions?

Diarrhea is often a source of trouble to dog owners. Consider parasites (worms) as a cause and eliminate this possibility first. Then, before trying anything more drastic, give careful thought to what you are feeding. Diet is the most common cause of diarrhea. Guard against:

1. Too much milk.
2. Too much fat.
3. Dog meal or biscuit that is too coarse or too bulky.

Often an elimination process is required to find a proper combination of foods acceptable to the dog's intestinal tract.

If diarrhea persists after taking these steps, your veterinarian will examine and check your dog for bacterial infection.

When will my female have her first heat period?

There is a variation in heat cycles. Generally our Springers come in season for the first time at about 9 months (it can be as early as 6 or as late as 11 months). The heat period lasts about 18 days and occurs again at 6-month intervals for the remainder of her life. There is no menopause in a dog.

When should I breed her?

We suggest her second heat period unless the bitch has come in season late, is well developed and in excellent health. It is best to skip a season before breeding her again.

Is it wrong to consider spaying her?

If you have no desire to raise a litter of puppies, or to ever show your female—if she is only to be your pet and companion, we urge you to have her unsexed. This is better than risking the likely possibility of a mismating to some roaming neighborhood male.

My dog came back from a boarding kennel yesterday and seems to have a bone caught in his throat. He is feeling fine—full of pep, eating well and his stools are good—but he sometimes raises a little mucus or liquid when he coughs. Do you think this is serious?

Your dog has symptoms of what we commonly call "kennel cough", properly *tracho-bronchitis* (an upper respiratory disease) or *para-influenza*. Animals infected with this virus usually recover in about two weeks. I suggest you ask your veterinarian.

In answering the above questions, we have tried to pass on what we have learned as a long-time dog breeder and raiser. But in no way do we advocate the administering to your puppies and adult dogs as a do-it-yourself operation. Let your veterinarian be your dependable guide.

1. Let me know if you catch anything . . .

2. Yes, that's a fish on your line . . .

3. Easy with the reel now . . .

4. Watch it—you're losing it . . .

5. There it goes . . .

6. Oh well, let's just watch them swim.

Good mover—side view

20

Official Standard for The English Springer Spaniel

(Approved by the Directors of The American Kennel Club in August 1956)

General Appearance and Type:

The English Springer Spaniel is a medium-size sporting dog with a neat, compact body, and a docked tail. His coat is moderately long, glossy, usually liver and white or black and white, with feathering on his legs, ears, chest and brisket.

His pendulous ears, soft gentle expression, sturdy build and friendly wagging tail proclaim him unmistakably a member of the ancient family of spaniels. He is above all a well proportioned dog, free from exaggeration, nicely balanced in every part.

His carriage is proud and upstanding, body deep, legs strong and muscular with enough length to carry him with ease. His short level back, well developed thighs, good shoulders, excellent feet, suggest power, endurance, agility.

Taken as a whole he looks the part of a dog that can go and keep going under difficult hunting conditions, and moreover he enjoys what he is doing. At his best he is endowed with style, symmetry, balance, enthusiasm and is every inch a sporting dog of distinct spaniel character, combining beauty and utility.

To be penalized: Those lacking true English Springer type in conformation, expression, or behavior.

Temperament:

The typical Springer is friendly, eager to please, quick to learn, willing to obey. In the show ring he should exhibit poise, attentiveness, tractability, and should permit himself to be examined by the judge without resentment or cringing.

To be penalized: Excessive timidity, with due allowance for puppies and novice exhibits. But no dog to receive a ribbon if he behaves in vicious manner toward handler or judge. Aggressiveness toward other dogs in the ring NOT *to be construed as viciousness.*

Size and Proportion:

The Springer is built to cover rough ground with agility and reasonable speed. He should be kept to medium size—neither too small nor too large and heavy to do the work for which he is intended.

The ideal shoulder height for dogs is 20 inches; for bitches, 19 inches.

Length of topline (the distance from top of the shoulders to the root of the tail) should be approximately equal to the dog's shoulder height—never longer than his height—and not appreciably less. The dog too long in body, especially when long in loin, tires easily and lacks the compact outline characteristic of the breed.

Equally undesirable is the dog too short in body for the length of his legs, a condition that destroys his balance and restricts the gait.

Weight is dependent on the dog's other dimensions: a 20 inch dog, well proportioned, in good condition should weigh about 49–55 pounds. The resulting appearance is a well knit, sturdy dog with good but not too heavy bone, in no way coarse or ponderous.

To be penalized: Over-heavy specimens, cloddy in build. Leggy individuals, too tall for their length and substance. Over-size or under-size specimens (those more than one inch under or over the breed ideal).

Color and Coat:

Color may be liver or black with white markings; liver and white (or black and white) with tan markings; blue or liver roan; or predominantly white with tan, black or liver markings.

On ears, chest, legs and belly the Springer is nicely furnished with a fringe of feathering (of moderate heaviness).

On his head, front or forelegs, and below hocks on front of hindlegs the hair is short and fine.

The body coat is flat or wavy, of medium length, sufficiently dense to be water-proof, weather-proof and thorn-proof.

The texture fine, and the hair should have the clean, glossy, live appearance indicative of good health.

It is legitimate to trim about head, feet, ears; to remove dead hair; to thin and shorten excess feathering particularly from the hocks to the feet and elsewhere as required to give a smart, clean appearance.

To be penalized: Rough curly coat. Over-trimming, especially of the body coat. Any chopped, barbered, or artificial effect. Excessive feathering that destroys the clean outline desirable in a sporting dog. Off colors such as lemon, red, or orange not to place.

Head:

The head is impressive without being heavy. Its beauty lies in a combination of strength and refinement. It is important that the size and proportion be in balance with the rest of the dog. Viewed in profile the head should appear approximately the same length as the neck and should blend with the body in substance.

The skull (upper head) to be of medium length, fairly broad, flat on top, slightly rounded at the sides and back. The occiput bone inconspicuous, rounded rather than peaked or angular.

The foreface (head in front of the eyes) approximately the same length as the skull, and in harmony as to width and general character.

Looking down on the head, the muzzle to appear to be about one-half the width of the skull. As the skull rises from the foreface it makes a brow or "stop," divided by a groove or fluting between the eyes. This groove continues upward and gradually disappears as it reaches the middle of the forehead.

The amount of "stop" can best be described as moderate. It must not be a pronounced feature as in the Clumber Spaniel. Rather it is a subtle rise where the muzzle blends into the upper head, further emphasized by the groove and by the position and shape of the eyebrows which should be well-developed. The stop, eyebrows and the chiseling of the bony structure around the eye sockets contribute to the Springer's beautiful and characteristic expression.

Viewed in profile, the topline of the skull and the muzzle lie in two approximately parallel planes. The nasal bone should be straight, with no inclination downward toward the tip of the nose which gives a down-faced look so undesirable in this breed. Neither should the nasal bone be concave resulting in a "dish-faced" profile; nor convex giving the dog a "Roman nose."

The jaws to be of sufficient length to allow the dog to carry game easily; fairly square, lean, strong, and even (neither undershot nor overshot).

The upper lip to come down full and rather square to cover the line of the lower jaw, but lips not to be pendulous nor exaggerated.

The nostrils, well opened and broad, liver color or black depending on the color of the coat. Flesh-colored ("Dudley noses") or spotted ("butterfly noses") are undesirable. The cheeks to be flat (not rounded, full, or thick), with nice chiseling under the eyes.

To be penalized: Oval, pointed, or heavy skull. Cheeks prominently rounded, thick and protruding. Too much or too little stop. Over-heavy muzzle. Muzzle too short, too thin, too narrow. Pendulous, slobbery lips. Under- or over-shot jaws—a very serious fault, to be heavily penalized.

Teeth:

The teeth should be strong, clean, not too small; and when the mouth is closed the teeth should meet in an even bite or a close scissors bite (the lower incisors touching the inside of the upper incisors).

To be penalized: Any deviation from above description. One or two teeth slightly out of line not to be considered a serious fault, but irregularities due to faulty jaw formation to be severely penalized.

Eyes:

More than any other feature the eyes contribute to the Springer's appeal. Color, placement, size influence expression and attractiveness. The eyes to be of medium size, neither small, round, full and prominent, nor bold and hard in expression. Set rather well apart and fairly deep in their sockets.

The color of the iris to harmonize with the color of the coat, preferably a good dark hazel in the liver dogs and black or deep brown in the black and white specimens.

The expression to be alert, kindly, trusting. The lids tight with little or no haw showing.

1. A bad head—Eyes too prominent—Narrow pointed skull
2. Heavy skull—Cheeky—High set ears
3. A well proportioned head

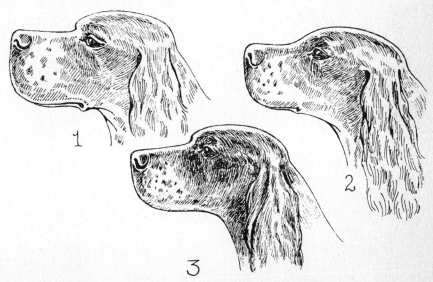

1. Too much stop—heavy lips—loose lidded eyes
2. Too little stop—muzzle too short for skull
3. A good head

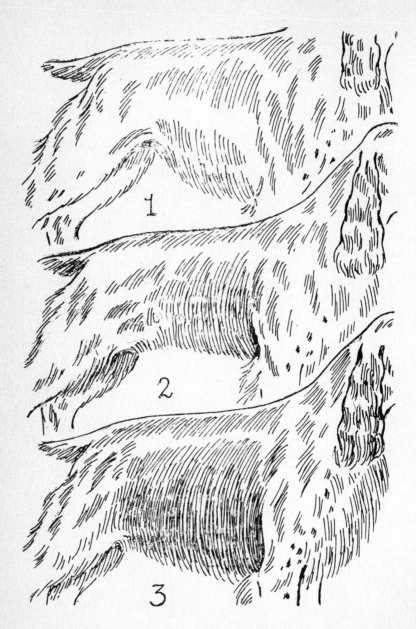

1. Too much tuck-up
2. Narrow rib section—Shallow
3. Good bottom line—No tuck-up

To be penalized: *Eyes yellow or brassy in color or noticeably lighter than the coat. Sharp expression indicating unfriendly or suspicious nature. Loose droopy lids. Prominent haw (the third eyelid or membrane in the inside corner of the eye).*

Ears:

The correct ear-set is on a level with the line of the eye; on the side of the skull and not too far back. The flaps to be long and fairly wide, hanging close to the cheeks, with no tendency to stand up or out. The leather thin, approximately long enough to reach the tip of the nose.

To be penalized: *Short round ears. Ears set too high or too low or too far back on the head.*

Neck:

The neck to be moderately long, muscular, slightly arched at the crest, gradually blending into sloping shoulders. Not noticeably upright nor coming into the body at an abrupt angle.

To be penalized: *Short neck, often the sequence to steep shoulders. Concave neck, sometimes called ewe neck or upside down neck (the opposite of arched). Excessive throatiness.*

Body:

The body to be well coupled, strong, compact; the chest deep but not so wide or round as to interfere with the action of the front legs; the brisket sufficiently developed to reach to the level of the elbows.

The ribs fairly long, springing gradually to the middle of the body, then tapering as they approach the end of the ribbed section.

The back (section between the withers and loin) to be straight and strong, with no tendency to dip or roach.

The loins to be strong, short; a slight arch over loins and hip bones. Hips nicely rounded, blending smoothly into hind legs.

The resulting topline slopes *very gently* from withers to tail—the line from withers to back descending without a sharp drop; the back practically level; arch over hips somewhat lower than the withers; croup sloping gently to base of tail; tail carried to follow the natural line of the body.

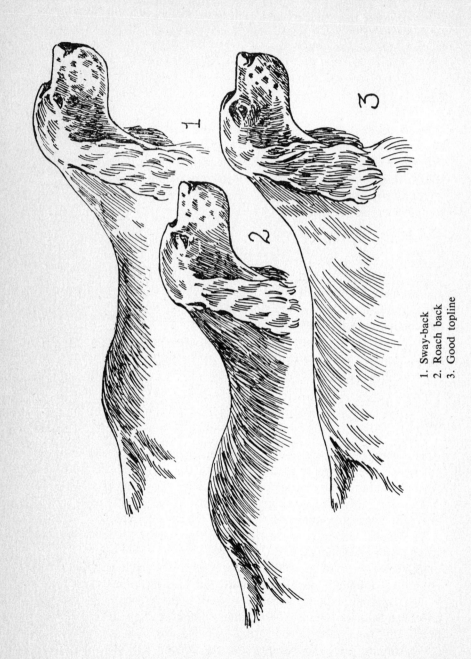

1. Sway-back
2. Roach back
3. Good topline

The bottom line, starting on a level with the elbows, to continue backward with almost no up-curve until reaching the end of the ribbed section, then a more noticeable upcurve to the flank, but not enough to make the dog appear small waisted or "tucked up."

To be penalized: Body too shallow, indicating lack of brisket. Ribs too flat—sometimes due to immaturity. Ribs too round (barrel-shaped), hampering the gait. Sway-back (dip in back), indicating weakness or lack of muscular development, particularly to be seen when dog is in action and viewed from the side. Roach back (too much arch over loin and extending forward into middle section).

Croup falling away too sharply; or croup too high—unsightly faults, detrimental to outline and good movement.

Topline sloping sharply, indicating steep withers (straight shoulder placement) and a too low tail-set.

Tail:

The Springer's tail is an index both to his temperament and his conformation. Merry tail action is characteristic. The proper set is somewhat low, following the natural line of the croup. The carriage should be nearly horizontal, slightly elevated, when dog is excited. Carried straight up is untypical of the breed.

The tail should not be docked too short and should be well fringed with wavy feather. It is legitimate to shape and shorten the feathering but enough should be left to blend with the dog's other furnishings.

To be penalized: Tail habitually upright. Tail set too high or too low. Clamped down tail (indicating timidity or undependable temperament, even less to be desired than the tail carried too gayly).

Forequarters:

Efficient movement in front calls for proper shoulders, the blades sloping back to form an angle with the forearm of approximately 90 degrees which permits the dog to swing his forelegs forward in an easy manner.

Shoulders (fairly close together at the tips) to lie flat and mold smoothly into the contour of the body.

The foreleg to be straight with the same degree of size to the foot. The bone, strong, slightly flattened, not too heavy or round. The knee

1. Too wide in front

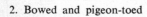

2. Bowed and pigeon-toed

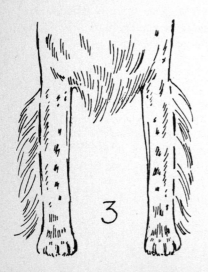

3. A good front

straight, almost flat; the pasterns short, strong; elbows close to the body with free action from the shoulders.

To be penalized: Shoulders set at a steep angle limiting the stride. Loaded shoulders (the blades standing out from the body by overdevelopment of the muscles). Loose elbows, crooked legs. Bone too light or too coarse and heavy. Weak pasterns that let down the feet at a pronounced angle.

Hindquarters:

The Springer should be shown in hard muscular condition, well developed in hips and thighs and the whole rear assembly should suggest strength and driving power.

The hip joints to be set rather wide apart and the hips nicely rounded. The thighs broad and muscular; the stifle joint strong and moderately bent. The hock joint somewhat rounded, not small and sharp in contour, and moderately angulated. Leg from hock joint to foot pad, short and strong with good bone structure.

When viewed from the rear the hocks to be parallel whether the dog is standing or in motion.

To be penalized: Too little or too much angulation. Narrow, undeveloped thighs. Hocks too short or too long (a proportion of 1/3 the distance from hip joint to foot is ideal). Flabby muscles. Weakness of joints.

Feet:

The feet to be round, or slightly oval, compact, well arched, medium size with thick pads, well feathered between the toes. Excess hair to be removed to show the natural shape and size of the foot.

To be penalized: Thin, open, or splayed feet (flat with spreading toes). Hare foot (long, rather narrow foot).

Movement:

In judging the Springer there should be emphasis on proper movement which is the final test of a dog's conformation and soundness. Prerequisite to good movement is balance of the front and rear assemblies.

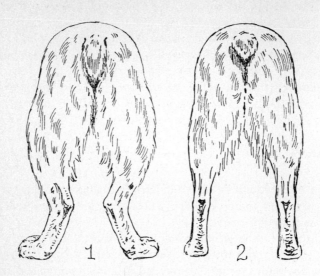

1. Cowhocks
2. Good rear

1. Good side rear
2. Thigh too narrow—not enough angulation.
   Hocks too long and sharp

The two must match in angulation and muscular development if the gait is to be smooth and effortless.

Good shoulders laid back at an angle that permits a long stride are just as essential as the excellent rear quarters that provide the driving power.

When viewed from the front the dog's legs should appear to swing forward in a free and easy manner, with no tendency for the feet to cross over or interfere with each other. Viewed from the rear the hocks should drive well under the body following on a line with the forelegs, the rear legs parallel, neither too widely nor too closely spaced.

Seen from the side the Springer should exhibit a good long forward stride, without high-stepping or wasted motion.

To be penalized: Short choppy stride, mincing steps with up and down movement, hopping. Moving with forefeet wide, giving roll or swing to body. Weaving or crossing of forefeet or hind feet. Cowhocks—hocks turning in toward each other.

In judging the English Springer Spaniel *the overall picture* is a primary consideration. It is urged that the judge look for *type* which includes general appearance, outline, and temperament, and also for *soundness,* especially as seen when the dog is in motion.

Inasmuch as the dog with a smooth easy gait must be reasonably sound and *well balanced* he is to be highly regarded in the show ring, however, not to the extent of forgiving him for not looking like an English Springer Spaniel.

A quite untypical dog, leggy, foreign in head and expression, may move well. But he should not be placed over a good all-round specimen that has a minor fault in movement.

It should be remembered that the English Springer Spaniel is first and foremost a sporting dog of the spaniel family and he must look and behave and move in character.

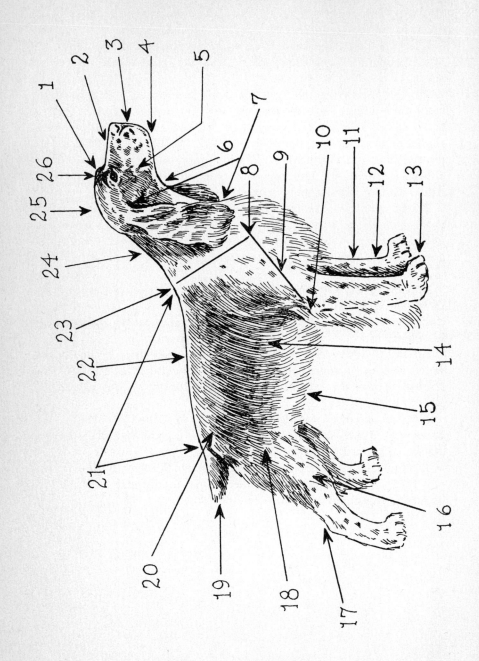

KEY TO ENGLISH SPRINGER SPANIEL CHART

1—Stop, moderate; eyebrows, well developed
2—Nasal bone, straight
3—Muzzle, fairly square
4—Jaws, strong, even
5—Chiseling under eyes
6—Not too throaty
7—Ears, set low, falling close to head
8—Sloping shoulders
9—Brisket to elbow
10—Elbows, close to body
11—Forelegs, straight with good bone, slightly flattened
12—Pasterns, strong
13—Feet, strong, compact, toes arched, pads thick
14—Body, deep, ribs well sprung

15—Not tucked up
16—Stifle joint, strong, moderately bent
17—Hock joint, rounded, moderately bent, well let down
18—Thighs, broad, muscular
19—Tail, set low, carried horizontally with merry action
20—Hips, nicely rounded
21—Distance withers to base of tail, slightly less than shoulder height
22—Back, strong, no dip or roach
23—Shoulder blades, fairly close
24—Neck, arched
25—Occiput bone, rounded, inconspicuous
26—Eyes, dark, friendly, tight lids

INDEX TO PEDIGREES

A rare photo of the two greatest show-winning English Springer Spaniels of all time together. Ch. Chinoe's Adamant James (see page 212) is at left with handler Clint Harris, and his sire Ch. Salilyn's Aristocrat (page 195) is at right with Barbara Gates, following their appearance in a special exhibition at the Detroit Kennel Club show in March, 1972. "D–J", who was four years old at time of the photo, and "Risto" who was seven, never met in actual competition.